GRILLED
TO PERFECTION

GRILLED
TO PERFECTION

PETER HOWARD

Photography by Jo Gamvros

NH
NEW
HOLLAND

TO ALL MY FAMILY

THE DEDICATION TO MY FAMILY REFLECTS THE WONDERFUL TIMES WE HAVE HAD AROUND BARBECUES. MY DAD AND MUM, KEITH AND DOROTHY, AND MY SIBLINGS — KERRY-ANNE, PAUL, MADONNA, MAREE AND PATRICK — ALL LOVE A GOOD GET-TOGETHER. AND GENERALLY THOSE GET-TOGETHERS TOOK PLACE AROUND THE BARBECUE THAT MY DAD BUILT FOR US.

MY THANKS GO TO BRENDA OAKLEY, WHO HAS ONCE AGAIN BEEN MY RIGHT-HAND WITH THIS BOOK (FOR THE THIRD TIME) AND TO JANE PARVIAINEN WHO HELPED ME TEST THE RECIPES. IT IS SO GOOD TO BE WORKING WITH MY MATES AT NEW HOLLAND.

OVER THE LAST TEN YEARS OR SO, I HAVE COME TO RESPECT THE RESILIENCE AND GENEROSITY OF THE AUSTRALIAN PRIMARY PRODUCERS WHO SUPPLY US WITH SO MUCH OUTSTANDING PRODUCE, AND MY THANKS MUST GO TO THEM. LASTLY, THANKS TO ALL OF YOU WHO HELPED TO MAKE *BARBECUED!* SO EXTREMELY POPULAR, NOT ONLY IN AUSTRALIA BUT ALSO IN THE UNITED KINGDOM, THE UNITED STATES AND CANADA.

conten

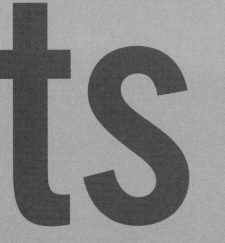

ts

introdu

Cooking on barbecues is nothing new, and it would appear that more and more of us are adopting this versatile way of cooking. It has been some time since I wrote *Barbecued!* (actually, nearly 4 years ago), and in that time, I have met many avid 'barbecuers' who have been following not only the recipes in that book but also the recipes in numerous other books that came out around the same time.

There can be no doubt that the 'cremation' period is over — well, let's hope so! We now have barbecues that let us cook well without over-crisping and burning everything that goes near them! No more greasy, cremated mess masquerading as dinner … or lunch or even breakfast!

I have once again written for a simple gas barbecue with some handy extras, such as the stainless steel bowl or the lid of the wok which allow you to cook thicker pieces of meat or whatever, more quickly. My Dad had one favourite accessory for his barbecue — an enamel pie dish which allowed him to partially steam or barbecue thicker food items to retain their juiciness, not to mention his sensational barbecued onions (see page 114 of *Barbecued!*).

I rejoice at the number of women who have been coming to the barbecue classes that developed from *Barbecued!* I have often thought it was a silly sexist attitude that only men barbecued. It's nonsense, of course; everyone can enjoy this delicious and relaxed way of cooking. It is attracting an increasing number of devotees as we become more time-poor — working harder and seeing friends and family less frequently than we would like to. A barbecue means we can socialise as we cook and chat with our friends or family.

ction

Barbecuing is a method of cooking where maximum results can be achieved with minimum effort if you use as little oil as possible and so allow all the natural flavours to shine through — and good produce is all about natural flavours.

I recently moved house, and the first item of furniture (if it can be called that) to be unpacked was the barbecue. It now sits in pride of place and, because it is so accessible, is in constant use. However, you don't need a barbecue that takes up a lot of space. Smaller barbecues are fine to get that grilling going. And why not? You can cook equally well on these.

Inside everyone who loves good food, there is a barbecuer. This book is written for all those folk who already love this method of cooking and for all those who want to know more about it.

Once again, enjoy!

Peter Howard

laws of ba

1. ALWAYS START WITH A CLEAN BARBECUE PLATE. AFTER YOU FINISH COOKING, CLEAN IT SO IT IS READY FOR NEXT TIME.

2. HEAT YOUR BARBECUE TO THE REQUIRED TEMPERATURE WELL BEFORE USE. AT THE START OF EACH RECIPE, I GIVE THE TEMPERATURE AND SECTION OF THE BARBECUE TO BE USED.

3. CONCENTRATE ON YOUR COOKING SO THAT YOU NEVER END UP WITH A CHARRED MESS. USE THE RECIPES AS A GUIDE AND FEEL FREE TO ALTER THE INGREDIENTS TO SUIT YOUR PERSONAL TASTES.

4. ALWAYS BE CAREFUL WHEN HANDLING FOOD. FOR EXAMPLE, DON'T LEAVE RAW INGREDIENTS SITTING IN THE SUN, NEVER LET RAW MEAT OR ITS JUICES COME INTO CONTACT WITH COOKED MEAT, AND NEVER USE LEFTOVER MARINADE AS A SAUCE WITHOUT COOKING IT FIRST.

5. DON'T MASK THE NATURAL FLAVOURS OF YOUR INGREDIENTS WITH TOO MANY ADDITIONS — LET THEM SHINE THROUGH.

6. WHILE YOU SHOULDN'T BE AFRAID TO TRY SOMETHING NEW, DON'T FORGET THAT SPONGE CAKES AND SOUFFLÉS ARE NOT MEANT TO BE COOKED ON THE BARBECUE. SPICE YOUR CULINARY AMBITIONS WITH REALISM!

7. HAVE THE APPROPRIATE UTENSILS READY — TONGS OR WHATEVER IMPLEMENTS YOU NEED — BEFORE YOU START COOKING ON THE BARBECUE.

8. ENSURE THAT THE GAS TANK IS FILLED. THIS SAVES YOU FROM THE ULTIMATE EMBARRASSMENT OF RUNNING OUT OF PUFF BEFORE THE MEAL IS COOKED.

9. AS THE BARBECUE IS OFTEN THE CENTRE FOR FAMILY ENTERTAINMENT, BE AWARE OF THE MOVEMENTS OF ANY CHILDREN AROUND WHILE YOU ARE COOKING.

10. THE LAST LAW IS SIMPLE — ENJOY YOURSELF! A BARBECUE ALWAYS SEEMS TO ATTRACT GOOD HUMOUR AND GREAT FRIENDS. WITH CAREFUL PREPARATION THERE IS NOTHING LEFT FOR YOU TO DO BUT TO COOK AND ENJOY!

to

start

ASPARAGUS ON HORSEBACK

Asparagus and ham are a simple, but classic combination. With the many different kinds of ham now available, you can achieve many flavour variations. Whichever type of ham you decide to use, though, always combine it with fresh asparagus.

Serves 4
Temperature: medium
Section of barbecue used: open slats

16 asparagus spears
8 slices Parma ham
olive oil spray
extra virgin olive oil
cracked pepper (optional)

IN THE KITCHEN

Trim the asparagus spears — the best point to break them is where the spears turn pale.

Cut the Parma ham slices in half and wrap each half around an asparagus spear, starting from the bottom and winding up to the top. Refrigerate until ready to use.

AT THE BARBECUE

Spray the Parma ham-wrapped asparagus lightly with oil and put on the barbecue. Turn constantly for a minute or two, until the ham starts to go crisp and pale.

AT THE TABLE

Place the Parma ham-wrapped asparagus on a platter and drizzle over a very small amount of extra virgin olive oil; sprinkle over cracked pepper if you like. You can serve standing around the barbecue area or at the table.

THAI-STYLE CHICKEN CAKES

I have used breadcrumbs here — which would never be used
in a Thai household — to soak up some of the moisture.

Makes 15–20 cakes
Temperature: medium
Section of barbecue used: flat plate

500g (1lb) chicken thigh fillets

1 red pepper, chopped

2 red chillies, chopped

2 cloves garlic, chopped

1 tablespoon grated root ginger

1 lemongrass stalk, tender part only,
 chopped

2 Kaffir lime leaves, shredded

1 tablespoon Thai fish sauce (*nam pla*)

125ml (4fl oz) coconut milk

1 whole egg

125g (4oz) green beans, cut into
 3mm ($1/8$in) slices

250g (8oz) fresh breadcrumbs

4 tablespoons vegetable or peanut oil

250ml (8fl oz) Thai Cucumber Sauce
 (see recipe page 135)

IN THE KITCHEN

Cut chicken into small pieces. Combine the red pepper, chillies,
garlic, ginger, lemon grass, Kaffir leaves and fish sauce in a
food processor (or use a mortar and pestle) and blend to a
smooth paste.

Add chicken pieces, coconut milk and egg and blend well.
Place mixture in a bowl and add sliced beans.

Chill for at least 1 hour, then stir in the breadcrumbs to take
up some of the excess moisture.

AT THE BARBECUE

Pour on half the oil. Add a half-tablespoon of the chicken
mixture to the plate. Don't try and do too many chicken
cakes at one time as they cook quickly; 6 at a time is plenty.

When you are ready to flip the half-cooked cakes over
(usually after 1–2 minutes), make sure the plate is oiled.
Flip them over to cook through using the remaining oil.
Repeat until all the mixture has gone.

Lift cakes off the barbecue and place them on a plate lined
with kitchen paper to drain and cool.

AT THE TABLE

Serve on a platter with the Thai Cucumber Sauce on the side.

BACON, CHILLI JAM AND PEANUT BUTTER ROLLS

Makes 12
Temperature: hot
Section of barbecue used: open slats

6 slices fresh white or brown bread
smooth peanut butter
spreadable chilli jam
4–6 bacon rashers, rinds removed
   and cut into equal pieces
thick cocktail sticks
olive oil spray

IN THE KITCHEN

Cut the crusts from the bread, spread with peanut butter and smear with chilli jam (if the jam is not all that spreadable, warm it in the microwave for 5–10 seconds). Then cut each slice into two even rectangles.

Roll up the bread rectangles and then roll a piece of bacon around each of them; secure with a cocktail stick and repeat the process until all the slices are done.

AT THE BARBECUE

Spray the bacon-wrapped rolls with oil and place on the barbecue. Turn rolls regularly to crisp the bacon and heat the rolls.

AT THE TABLE

Serve to guests while standing around the barbecue or at the table with napkins.

CHARDONNAY BUTTER OYSTERS

Chardonnay, butter and oysters — the flavours of each are synonymous with fine dining. Like many other fantastic combinations, it is very simple to put them all together successfully.

Serves 4
Temperature: high
Section of barbecue used: open slats

48 opened oysters, on the shell
250ml (8fl oz) Chardonnay wine
2 green spring onions
1 teaspoon ground black pepper
250g (8oz) unsalted butter, diced
3-4 tablespoons chopped parsley

IN THE KITCHEN
Make sure the oysters are washed and clean.
Pour the wine into a saucepan and bring to the boil. Meanwhile, trim and finely chop the spring onions, add them to the wine along with the pepper and simmer for 2 minutes. Remove from the heat and swirl in the butter to melt and combine with the wine.

AT THE BARBECUE
Put the oysters on the open slats about 6–8 at a time. Spoon some of the butter mixture over them and sprinkle over the chopped parsley. The liquid needs to be just bubbling to indicate the oysters are ready to serve. Do not boil or overcook as they shrink easily.

AT THE TABLE
These oysters are best served around the barbecue. Lift them onto napkins and offer to family and guests. The oysters easily slip out of the shell and onto the tongue. Have a container handy to take the empty shells.

If you have any butter mixture left over, store it for use later over fish or chicken. Reheat it in a saucepan or in the microwave.

SKEWERED PRAWNS WITH ORIENTAL SLAW

Prawns make a popular barbecue appetizer choice.

Serves 4
Temperature: medium
Section of barbecue used: flat plate

12 large raw tiger prawns

4 fresh pineapple slices

4–8 lemongrass stalks, approximately
    20cm (8in) long

125ml (4fl oz) light soy sauce

$^1/_2$ teaspoon sesame oil

SLAW

$^1/_2$ Chinese cabbage

2 small shallots, peeled and finely sliced

1 clove garlic, crushed

1 green pepper, finely sliced

1 large green chilli, deseeded and cut thinly into
    half moons

60g ($2^1/_2$oz) roasted cashews, roughly chopped

DRESSING

juice of 2 limes

125ml (4fl oz) vegetable oil

2 tablespoons palm sugar

2–3 tablespoons Thai fish sauce, (to taste)
    (*nam pla*)

8 lime wedges

IN THE KITCHEN

Peel and devein the prawns. Cut the pineapple slices into half moons, remove the core and cut pineapple into V-shaped pieces.

Taper the lemongrass to use as skewers — I generally use the root end and sharpen that part to make it easier to thread on the food. Pierce each piece of pineapple with a sharp knife to make the process easier and then thread the prawns and pineapple alternatively onto the lemongrass.

Refrigerate skewers until ready. Mix the soy sauce and sesame oil together and set aside.

Remove and discard the core from the cabbage then wash the leaves, shake dry and shred. Put into a bowl and add the shallots, garlic, green pepper, chilli and cashews.

Whisk the lime juice, vegetable oil, sugar and fish sauce together and pour over the cabbage. Toss to coat and refrigerate for 30 minutes before use.

AT THE BARBECUE

Brush the prawn skewers with the soy and sesame oil and put on the barbecue plate. Baste with the soy and sesame oil and turn gently until the prawns lose their transparency, about 6-8 minutes.

AT THE TABLE

Toss the slaw and put on a platter. Slightly flatten the slaw, then place the prawn skewers on top. Serve with lime wedges.

BARBECUED CHEESE

This is a marvellous way to serve strongly flavoured firm cheeses.

Serves 4
Temperature: medium
Section of barbecue used: flat plate

12 shards/triangles, approximately
 1cm ($^1/_2$in) thick (60g/2oz each)
 hard cheese such as Parmesan or
 Gruyère (or halloumi)
cold water
125g (4oz) plain flour
olive oil spray
mixed salad leaves
few sprigs flat-leaf parsley, to garnish
1 lemon, quartered

IN THE KITCHEN
Dip each shard/triangle into the cold water, shake off the excess and then dust in flour.

AT THE BARBECUE
Spray the flat plate liberally with oil and put on the cheese. Cook each shard/triangle for about 30–60 seconds on each side or until golden brown. Remove from heat immediately.

AT THE TABLE
Put the salad leaves in the middle of a serving plate, add the cheese and top with a little parsley. Serve with lemon quarters.

CRISPY FOCACCIA WITH SPICY BLACK-EYED BEAN PASTE AND ROCKET SALAD

Serves 4

Temperature: high

Section of barbecue used: open slats

2 good-sized pieces focaccia

125g (4oz) rocket leaves

garlic-infused oil

225g (8oz) Spicy Black-Eyed Bean Paste
   (see recipe page 134)

1 red pepper, diced

60g (2^1/$_2$oz) sun-dried tomatoes, roughly
   chopped

45g (1^1/$_4$oz) Pecorino Romano cheese,
   roughly grated/sliced

extra virgin olive oil

cracked lemon pepper

IN THE KITCHEN

Cut the focaccia through the middle to give 4 even squares or rectangles.

Make sure the rocket is washed and crisp.

AT THE BARBECUE

Sprinkle the focaccia with garlic oil, then brown and crisp both sides on the open slats.

AT THE TABLE

Spread the cut sides of the focaccia thickly with the Spicy Black-Eyed Bean Paste. Heap rocket leaves on top of the paste — don't worry if some of them slip off. Sprinkle equal quantities of red pepper, sun-dried tomato and cheese over the top, then drizzle over a little oil and finish off with a sprinkle of pepper. Serve immediately.

HAM, CUMIN AND COUSCOUS CAKES

Makes 16–18 cakes
Temperature: low/medium
Section of barbecue used: flat plate

60g (2$\frac{1}{2}$oz) ham, finely minced
1 tablespoon finely chopped spring onions
2 cloves garlic, crushed
rehydrated couscous (250g/9oz dried
   couscous mixed with 250ml/8fl oz boiling
   water)
1 teaspoon cumin powder
1 egg, beaten
1 tablespoon plain flour
1 teaspoon salt
1 tablespoon chopped chives
olive oil spray for barbecuing
sour cream (optional)

IN THE KITCHEN

Mix all the ingredients together except for the oil and sour cream and refrigerate for at least 1 hour before use.

With wet hands, take a tablespoon of the mixture and roll into a ball, then flatten slightly — this allows it to cook evenly.

AT THE BARBECUE

Oil the flat plate well and add the cakes, cook on both sides until browning and starting to crisp (usually takes 2 minutes each side).

AT THE TABLE

Put the cakes onto a platter and allow to cool before passing them around. If you want to serve them with sour cream, the cakes need to be quite cool because if they're too hot, the cream melts. Only place half a teaspoon of cream (if that) on top of each cake.

HONEY AND CINNAMON BABA GANOUSH

Makes 400g (14oz)
Temperature: medium
Section of barbecue used: open slats

4 aubergines, around 300g (10oz) each,
    cut in half lengthways
vegetable oil
5 cloves garlic
1 teaspoon salt
100g ($3^{1}/_{4}$oz) tahini
60ml (2fl oz) lemon juice
2 tablespoons honey, warmed
1 teaspoon ground cinnamon
lightly barbecued Turkish bread, to serve
salad of your choice, to serve

IN THE KITCHEN

Cut diamond-shaped slits in the cut sides of the aubergine halves and then brush them with oil.

After cooking (see below) and cooling the aubergines, peel the skin away from the cooked flesh. Put the peeled flesh into a food processor with the garlic, salt, tahini, lemon juice, honey and cinnamon. Process into a smooth paste, remove from the bowl and keep warm.

AT THE BARBECUE

Put the aubergine flesh-side down on the open slats and cook, turning regularly, for 30 minutes or until the flesh is soft and coming away from the skin. Remove from heat and cool.

AT THE TABLE

This dish is best served with lightly barbecued Turkish bread (see recipe page 94) and salad.

Baba ganoush can be stored in the refrigerator for up to 7 days.

CURRIED COURGETTE POPPADOM STACKS

Serves 4

Temperature: medium/high

Section of barbecue used:

   flat plate/open slats

4 medium yellow courgettes

3 tablespoons vegetable oil

1 teaspoon black mustard seeds

1 tablespoon Indian curry powder

1 red pepper

1 small onion, peeled and diced

olive oil spray

12 small poppadoms

salt to taste

120ml (4fl oz) Indian mango pickle

250ml (8oz) plain yoghurt

IN THE KITCHEN

Trim the courgettes and cut down their centres lengthwise. Cut these halves into half-moon shapes around 2cm (¾in) long.

Pour the oil into a bowl and mix in the mustard seeds and curry powder. Dice the red pepper and add it with the onion to the oil mixture. Add the courgettes and toss to coat. Leave to sit for 1 hour before cooking.

AT THE BARBECUE

Spray both sides of the poppadoms liberally with oil and put them on the open slats two at a time. They crisp and sizzle very quickly so be ready to turn them over. Lift and drain them on kitchen paper.

Tip the courgette mixture onto the flat plate. Allow it cook through, turning regularly. The courgette is cooked when soft but still holding together. Sprinkle with salt to taste.

AT THE TABLE

In the centre of each guest's plate, put a little juice from the courgettes and then one poppadom. Spoon over some courgette mixture and add another poppadom; spoon over a little more of the courgettes and top with a poppadom. Repeat until all four plates are complete. Serve with the Indian mango pickle and yoghurt on the side.

JAPANESE SPICED FISH GOUJONS

Ever since I began cooking, spices have fascinated me. I have been fortunate enough to visit many markets around the world, and none was more exciting and exotic than the spice souq of Dubai. Multicultural influences on cooking have exploded — which definitely means spices.

Serves 4
Temperature: medium
Section of barbecue used: flat plate

400g (12oz) tuna fillets, skin removed
shichimi togarashi (Japanese spice mix)
150ml (5fl oz) ponzu sauce
2 tablespoons lime juice
oil spray

IN THE KITCHEN

Cut the fillets into strips 2cm (¾in) wide by 6cm (2in) long. Lightly coat the strips with shichimi togarashi and pat the spice mix into them. Cover and refrigerate for no more than 10 minutes.

Mix the ponzu and lime juice together and pour into two small bowls that will sit on the serving platter.

AT THE BARBECUE

Spray the flat plate with oil and put on it the strips of fish. Sprinkle with a little more of the Japanese spice mix and turn each strip gently. Sprinkle on more spice mix and pat it on with the back of a spatula. Repeat this process until all sides have been sprinkled and the fish strips are cooked through.

Lift fish onto a plate lined with pieces of kitchen paper.

AT THE TABLE

The fish goujons are best served on a platter arranged around the bowls of dipping sauce. Pass the platter around and have plenty of napkins on hand.

KING PRAWNS IN MINT AND CHERVIL SAUCE

Serves 4
Temperature: hot
Section of barbecue used: open slats

16 medium-sized king prawns
2 tablespoons light olive oil
$1/2$ teaspoon each of salt and ground,
    lemon-flavoured black pepper
8 sprigs mint, freshly sliced at time
    of serving
125ml (4 fl oz) Mint and Chervil Sauce
    (see recipe page 130)

IN THE KITCHEN

Peel the prawns completely and devein them. Toss them in oil, salt and the lemon pepper and put aside for 15 minutes.

AT THE BARBECUE

Place the prawns on the barbecue and turn regularly — they only take about four minutes to cook through. Remove from the heat.

AT THE TABLE

Toss the prawns with the mint and add a little more pepper if you like. Serve on a platter in the middle of the table, and serve the sauce separately.

POTATO CAKES WITH TARRAGON, PEAS AND SMOKED SALMON

Potatoes are readily available and infinitely versatile. Here they form the basis of a simple, easy to make but elegant appetizer.

Serves 4
Temperature: medium
Section of barbecue used: flat plate

1kg (2lb) starchy potatoes
1 medium onion, peeled
160g (5$^1/_2$oz) frozen or fresh peas
1 tablespoon plain flour
4 tablespoons chopped fresh tarragon
salt and white pepper to taste
3 tablespoons light olive oil
4 teaspoons sour cream
8 slices smoked salmon
4 teaspoons salmon roe or lumpfish roe

IN THE KITCHEN

Wash and peel the potatoes. Grate potatoes and onion into a bowl and add the peas, flour, tarragon, salt and pepper. Mix well.

Make 4 cakes or patties by taking handfuls of the potato mix and squeezing out the liquid. Shape into flattish, round cakes.

AT THE BARBECUE

Pour 2 tablespoons of olive oil onto the plate and put the cakes on. When the base of the cakes is set (usually after 2 minutes of cooking, depending on thickness of cake), drizzle some oil over the tops of the cakes and flip them over. Press down on each cake with the back of the spatula, making sure the shape of the cakes remains round. Do not add any more oil but keep turning the cakes until cooked through.

Lift from the barbecue plate onto a platter lined with kitchen paper.

AT THE TABLE

Put a teaspoon of sour cream in the centre of each serving plate (the cream stops the cakes from sliding off) and top with a cake. On top of the cake, place 2 slices of smoked salmon, then top with a teaspoon of the salmon or lumpfish roe.

SKEWERED SEA TROUT AND MUSHROOMS

Serves 4

Temperature: medium

Section of barbecue used: flat plate

4 x 180g (6oz) thick slices sea trout, skin removed

12–14 button mushrooms (depending on the size of the mushrooms)

4–8 bamboo skewers, soaked in water overnight

olive oil spray

250ml (8fl oz) nam prik (see recipe page 131)

IN THE KITCHEN

Cut the fish into even-sized cubes. Cut the mushrooms into approximately the same size as the fish cubes or, if they are small enough, leave them whole. Thread the fish and mushrooms onto the skewers alternately, and refrigerate until ready to barbecue.

AT THE BARBECUE

Spray the skewers with oil and put them on the plate. Turn skewers until done — the fish is cooked when it flakes easily. Spray with more oil if necessary.

AT THE TABLE

Skewers are good served to guests standing around the barbecue. Serve them on a platter with a small bowl of nam prik for dipping. Skewers also make an excellent first course at the dinner table served with a good Oriental salad.

sea

BARBECUED PRAWNS WITH CELLOPHANE NOODLE SALAD 36

CHARGRILLED PRAWNS WITH APRICOT AND JICAMA SALSA 38

CHERMOULA–MARINATED ATLANTIC SALMON WITH CUCUMBER SALAD 39

PRAWNS AND DILL RISOTTO CAKES WITH GARLIC, WHITE WINE AND
  ANCHOVY CREAM 40

DEVILLED ATLANTIC SALMON 42

SWORDFISH ON A BED OF COURGETTES AND TOMATOES WITH PRAWN
  AND LIME BUTTER 43

CUTTLEFISH WITH SPICY ITALIAN SAUSAGE AND PINE NUT SALAD 44

SESAME SWORDFISH KEBABS WITH MANGO AND LIME SALSA 46

SNAPPER, CHICKEN AND SAUSAGE WITH COUSCOUS AND SAFFRON SAUCE 47

SCALLOPS WITH WHITE BEAN PUREE AND PANINI BRUSCHETTA 48

YELLOW FIN TUNA WITH POTATOES AND ROASTED RED PEPPER MAYO 50

ORANGE-INFUSED WHOLE SEA TROUT AND ORIENTAL SALAD 52

food

BARBECUED PRAWNS WITH CELLOPHANE NOODLE SALAD

The more I visited Thailand, the more I grew to love this salad. Now Thai cuisine is so popular everywhere, all the ingredients are readily available. Both components of this dish can be served individually.

Serves 4
Temperature: medium
Section of barbecue used: open slats

20 king prawns, peeled and tails removed
2 tablespoons pineapple juice, from
    fresh pineapple
2 tablespoons peanut or vegetable oil
1 tablespoon Thai fish sauce (*nam pla*)
1 clove garlic, crushed
1 tablespoon grated root ginger
1 teaspoon white sugar
Cellophane Noodle Salad (see recipe
    page 100)

IN THE KITCHEN

Devein the prawns (optional).

Squeeze the flesh of a peeled and chopped pineapple to extract the juice.

Mix all the remaining ingredients together — except for the Cellophane Noodle Salad — and add the prawns. Coat prawns well and allow to marinate for 20 minutes.

Make the Cellophane Noodle Salad.

AT THE BARBECUE

Barbecue the prawns on the open slats for approximately 1–2 minutes each side, depending on their size.

AT THE TABLE

Have the salad arranged on a large platter and top with the prawns. Serve immediately.

CHARGRILLED PRAWNS WITH APRICOT AND JICAMA SALSA

Serves 4
Temperature: medium
Section of barbecue used: open slats

16 large prawns, shells and heads
   removed
4 bamboo skewers, soaked in
   water overnight

APRICOT AND JICAMA SALSA

400g (14oz) firm apricot flesh

200g (7oz) jicama (yam bean) or celeriac

2 spring onions, trimmed

1 teaspoon jalapeño chilli, finely diced

1 small red pepper, deseeded and
   cut into fine strips

$1/2$ teaspoon ground cumin

3 tablespoons roughly chopped coriander

1 tablespoon vegetable oil

90ml ($2^1/_2$fl oz) lime juice

olive oil spray

salt, to taste

IN THE KITCHEN

Remove the veins from the backs of the prawns and thread 4 prawns onto each bamboo skewer.

Cut the apricot flesh into small cubes and place in a mixing bowl. Peel the jicama, cut into fine strips and add to the apricot. Finely slice the spring onions and add to the other two salsa ingredients, then add the chilli, red pepper, cumin, coriander, oil and lime juice. Stir well to combine, cover and chill well for 40 minutes before use.

AT THE BARBECUE

Spray the prawns well with oil and put onto the open slats. Sprinkle them with salt as you cook them. When done, lift prawns onto a plate.

AT THE TABLE

Heap the salsa in the middle of a round serving bowl and arrange the skewered, cooked prawns on top of the salsa.

CHERMOULA-MARINATED ATLANTIC SALMON WITH CUCUMBER SALAD

Serves 4

Temperature: high

Section of barbecue used:

flat plate/open slats

500g (1lb) Atlantic salmon (fillet, cutlet or steak), skin removed

125ml (4fl oz) Chermoula (see recipe page 124)

300g (10oz) cucumber

1 teaspoon sea salt

1 teaspoon sugar

60ml (2fl oz) white wine vinegar

2 tablespoons fennel seeds, crushed

8 asparagus spears

light olive oil

olive oil spray

mixed salad leaves

crusty bread, to serve

IN THE KITCHEN

Marinate the salmon in the chermoula for 10 minutes. Cut the fish into smaller pieces if you find it easier to handle.

Deseed the cucumber by cutting it down the middle lengthwise and scraping out the seeds with a teaspoon. Using a vegetable peeler, cut the cucumber into longish ribbons and put into a bowl. Add the salt, sugar, vinegar and fennel; stir, cover and refrigerate for one hour.

Trim the asparagus spears.

AT THE BARBECUE

Pour a couple of tablespoons of olive oil onto the flat plate. Put the salmon on, flesh-side down, and leave to cook for 1–2 minutes, depending on the thickness of the fish. Turn the fish making sure it remains on an oiled part of the barbecue plate. Cook for 1–2 minutes. Salmon is best cooked rare to medium; lift it from the plate when done and allow to cool. If you prefer the fish to be well done, cook it for another 2 minutes on each side.

Spray the asparagus with oil and cook on the open slats for 2–3 minutes; remove, cool and cut into bite-sized pieces.

AT THE TABLE

Place the mixed leaves on a large platter. Remove cucumber from its bowl and scatter across the top of the leaves. Flake the fish over the cucumber and leaves mixture, and finish off by pouring over any of the cucumber liquid. Serve with crusty bread.

PRAWNS AND DILL RISOTTO CAKES WITH GARLIC, WHITE WINE AND ANCHOVY CREAM

Serves 4

Temperature: medium

Section of barbecue used: open slats
and flat plate

8–12 jumbo prawns, shells on

400g (12oz) risotto, cooled
(see Your Everyday Risotto, page 136)

3 tablespoons dill, chopped

$1/2$ teaspoon lemon essence

breadcrumbs

250ml (8fl oz) Garlic, White Wine and
Anchovy Cream (see recipe page 126)

garlic-infused oil

2–4 tablespoons olive oil for risotto cakes

IN THE KITCHEN

Cut the prawns in half lengthwise, rinse them clean and refrigerate until you are ready to use them.

Mix the risotto with the dill and lemon essence, and divide into 8 evenly sized portions. With wet hands, roll into balls then roll in the breadcrumbs, flattening them slightly to allow for even cooking on the barbecue. Cover and refrigerate the cakes for at least 1 hour before cooking.

Have the Garlic, White Wine and Anchovy Cream ready; it may need reheating either in a saucepan or the microwave.

AT THE BARBECUE

Sprinkle the prawns with garlic-infused oil and put on the open slats. When the flesh side of the prawns is placed down on the slats, make sure it is well oiled. Cook the prawns, turning regularly.

Put the risotto cakes on the heated flat plate covered with 2 tablespoons of oil. Spoon the remaining oil onto the cakes as they cook. Turn every minute until browned and crisp.

AT THE TABLE

Serve the prawns on a platter. Serve the risotto cakes separately, along with the Garlic, White Wine and Anchovy Cream. A good salad completes this meal.

DEVILLED ATLANTIC SALMON

Serves 4

Temperature: medium

Section of barbecue used:
 open slats and flat plate

4 large or 8 small potatoes, preferably
 Désirée or a semi-waxy variety, with
 skin on

olive oil spray

aluminium foil to wrap potatoes

2 tablespoons Worcestershire sauce

2 tablespoons tomato ketchup

1 teaspoon caster sugar

$^1/_2$ teaspoon paprika

1 tablespoon dried English mustard

60ml (2fl oz) lemon juice

300g (10oz) skinless Atlantic salmon meat,
 roughly diced

60ml (4fl oz) plain yoghurt

60ml (4fl oz) Home-made Mayonnaise (see
 recipe page 128)

watercress sprigs to garnish

IN THE KITCHEN

Wash the potatoes and boil them until nearly done. Drain and cool potatoes. Spray the foil with oil on the shiny side, then wrap the potatoes in the foil, shiny-side innermost, and set aside.

Mix the Worcestershire sauce, tomato ketchup, sugar, paprika and mustard into a paste. Stir the lemon juice in with the salmon, add the Worcestershire sauce mixture and stir to coat the salmon. Set aside for 20 minutes.

AT THE BARBECUE

Put the potato parcel over the open slats and cook until done; use a sharp knife or a skewer to test that the potatoes are cooked through. The knife will go through smoothly without resistance when they are cooked.

Spray the flat plate well with oil and toss on the fish pieces quickly. Cook salmon to medium doneness; do not over-cook as it dries out and loses flavour. When finished, remove salmon from the plate and allow to cool.

AT THE TABLE

Mash the cooled salmon with the yoghurt and mayonnaise and set to one side.

Put the potatoes onto a serving platter or on individual plates and cut a deep cross into each potato through the foil. Using your thumbs and fingers, squeeze the potatoes up so they open out — blossom, if you like. Spread the flesh a little wider and spoon heaps of the salmon mixture over the potatoes and platter. Serve garnished with the watercress sprigs.

SWORDFISH ON A BED OF COURGETTES AND TOMATOES WITH PRAWN AND LIME BUTTER

Serves 4
Temperature: medium/high
Section of barbecue used: flat plate

4 x 180g (6oz) swordfish steaks, skin removed
ground black pepper
4 medium courgettes
4 Roma tomatoes
olive oil spray
sea salt, to taste
fresh thyme sprigs
Prawn and Lime Butter (see recipe page 120)
20 Kalamata olives

IN THE KITCHEN

Trim the fish if necessary and sprinkle with ground black pepper. Trim the courgettes. Halve courgettes and tomatoes lengthwise.

AT THE BARBECUE

Spray the courgette and tomato halves liberally with oil. Sprinkle with salt and put on the flat plate cut-side down. Cook until starting to brown then turn onto skin side. Cook for 3 minutes, adding the thyme leaves only to the cut side. Spray with a little more oil if necessary, turn once more and cook for a minute. Lift from the barbecue.

Spray the fish with oil and cook on the flat plate. When the fish steaks have turned white halfway up their sides, turn them over and cook through; cooking time depends on the thickness of each steak. Note that swordfish cooks very quickly and goes mushy if over-cooked. When the steaks are cooked through and feel firm to the press of your middle finger or tongs, lift them carefully from the barbecue.

AT THE TABLE

Place 2 courgette halves in the centre of each plate, top with 2 tomato halves and then the fish. Add slices of Prawn and Lime Butter (to taste) on top of the fish and arrange the olives around it.

CUTTLEFISH WITH SPICY ITALIAN SAUSAGE AND PINE NUT SALAD

Serves 4

Temperature: medium to high

Section of barbecue used: flat plate
and open slats

500g (1lb) cuttlefish, body only and
with cuttlebone removed

2 tablespoons extra virgin olive oil

250g (8oz) spicy Italian sausage,
around 3cm (1in) in diameter

50g (2oz) pine nuts, toasted

mesclun salad mix

20 cherry tomatoes, halved

2 tablespoons finely grated lemon rind

60ml (2fl oz) lemon juice

2 tablespoons finely chopped flat-leaf parsley

sea salt, to taste

60ml (2fl oz) olive oil

IN THE KITCHEN

Cut the cuttlefish open to form one large flat piece and trim. With a very sharp knife, score the flesh into diamond shapes. Cut into bite-sized pieces, place in a bowl and pour over the 2 tablespoons of virgin olive oil. Toss the cuttlefish in the oil and allow to rest for 15 minutes. If you wish to use later, refrigerate it.

Cut the sausage into rounds approximately 1cm (½in) thick.

Place the nuts, mesclun and tomato halves in a salad bowl and refrigerate.

AT THE BARBECUE

Put the cuttlefish on the flat plate with the scored side down. Toss once the scored side is lightly browned — cuttlefish cooks quickly and if overcooked becomes tough. Remove cuttlefish from the barbecue and put in a bowl. Add the lemon rind, lemon juice, parsley and sea salt; toss to coat and allow to cool.

Put the sausage slices on the open slats to crisp and turn brown. Remove from the barbecue when done, approximately 1–2 minutes on each cut side.

AT THE TABLE

Pour the 60ml (2fl oz) of olive oil over the salad mix and toss. Divide the sausage slices among individual plates, place some salad on top and arrange the pieces of the cuttlefish on top and around the salad.

SESAME SWORDFISH KEBABS WITH MANGO AND LIME SALSA

Serves 4
Temperature: high
Section of barbecue used: flat plate

500g (1lb) swordfish
4 stainless steel skewers, oiled
1 tablespoon sesame seeds
$^{1}/_{2}$ tablespoon sesame oil
1 tablespoon vegetable oil
1 tablespoon light soy sauce

MANGO AND LIME SALSA
200g (7oz) mango flesh, diced
90g (3oz) red onion, diced
60ml (2fl oz) lime juice
8 coriander leaves, roughly chopped
1 teaspoon Thai fish sauce (*nam pla*)
1 large green chilli, very finely chopped

coriander leaves to garnish

IN THE KITCHEN

Ensure skin is removed from the swordfish and cut into even-sized pieces — 3-cm/1-in cubes. Thread fish pieces onto skewers and refrigerate until ready to use.

Make a sesame baste by pounding sesame seeds in a mortar and pestle. When crushed, add the oils and soy sauce; mix well and set aside.

Make the salsa by gently tossing together the mango, onion, lime juice, coriander leaves, fish sauce and chilli. Set to one side.

AT THE BARBECUE

Brush the swordfish kebabs with the baste and place on the flat plate. Turn regularly and carefully, and continue to baste using a pastry brush. Cook for 1–2 minutes on each side.

AT THE TABLE

Serve the kebabs and salsa on a platter garnished with coriander leaves.

SNAPPER, CHICKEN AND SAUSAGE WITH COUSCOUS AND SAFFRON SAUCE

Saffron, reputed to be the world's most expensive spice, is a beautiful aromatic to use in cooking. In this dish, I have combined classic paella ingredients with North African ones, resulting in a sublime marriage of textures and flavours.

Serves 4
Temperature: medium/hot
Section of barbecue used: open slats and flat plate

4 x 100g (3 $^1/_2$oz) pieces snapper
4 x 100g (3 $^1/_2$oz) pieces boneless chicken thigh fillets
100g (3 $^1/_2$oz) chorizo (or similar spicy sausage)
100g (3 $^1/_2$oz) Israeli couscous

SAFFRON SAUCE
60g (2oz) spring onions, sliced
125ml (4fl oz) chicken stock
375ml (12fl oz) single cream
1 clove garlic, crushed
1 bay leaf
$^1/_2$ teaspoon saffron threads
3 tablespoons chopped parsley

oil spray
salt and ground black pepper, to taste
crusty bread, to serve

IN THE KITCHEN

Trim the fish and chicken and cut the sausage into rounds 3cm (1in) thick.

Place the couscous into a large pan of boiling salted water and cook for 12 minutes or until tender. Drain and keep warm. (If you are not going to use it immediately, rinse the cooked couscous in cold water, drain and then pour and toss some oil through to stop it sticking. It can then be reheated in the microwave.)

Make the sauce by putting the spring onions, stock, cream, garlic, bay leaf, saffron and parsley in a suitable saucepan, bring to the boil and reduce to a simmer until the sauce is reduced a little and light yellow in colour. Keep the sauce hot.

AT THE BARBECUE

Spray the fish and chicken with oil and place the fish on the flat plate and the chicken on the open slats. Cook until done, seasoning with salt and pepper as you cook. Put the sausage rounds on the flat plate and cook, turning regularly, for 2 minutes, then transfer onto the open slats for 30 seconds each side.

AT THE TABLE

Reheat the couscous if needed. Pour the hot sauce over the couscous and toss together. Check for seasoning and adjust if necessary. Transfer couscous to a large serving bowl and top with the pieces of fish, chicken and sausage. Serve with crusty bread.

SCALLOPS WITH WHITE BEAN PUREE AND PANINI BRUSCHETTA

Serves 4

Temperature: medium and high

Section of barbecue used: flat plate and open slats

12 large scallops

WHITE BEAN PUREE

200g (7oz) canned cannellini beans, drained
1 clove garlic
sea salt and cayenne pepper, to taste
60ml (2fl oz) olive oil

PANINI BRUSCHETTA

8 slices panini (or ciabatta)
oil spray
1 very ripe red tomato, halved

ground black pepper
extra virgin olive oil
fresh basil leaves

IN THE KITCHEN

Trim the scallops of the vein that runs around the side of each one. Refrigerate until ready for use.

Cover the beans with water. Add the garlic, salt and cayenne, and simmer for 15 minutes. Drain and tip into a food processor bowl. Start processing, pouring the oil in slowly so it is incorporated into a smooth paste. Remove bean purée from the bowl and keep warm. Refrigerate the bean purée if not using immediately.

AT THE BARBECUE

Spray the panini slices with oil and place on open slats. Turn to check they are lightly brown; note that panini brown quickly. When browned on both sides, lift from the barbecue and rub panini with the cut part of the tomato halves, squeezing the flesh so that some adheres to the panini.

Spray the scallops with oil and flash-cook them on the flat plate. Scallops cook extremely quickly, so turn them after 30 seconds to check they are sealed and browned. Remove immediately when cooked.

AT THE TABLE

If you have refrigerated the bean purée, reheat it in a microwave.

Divide the warm bean purée among the four plates, placing it in the centre of each plate. Place three scallops on top, sprinkle over a little ground black pepper, drizzle with a little extra virgin olive oil and garnish with fresh basil leaves. Serve the bruschetta in a bread basket.

YELLOW FIN TUNA WITH POTATOES AND ROASTED RED PEPPER MAYO

Serves 4

Temperature: medium

Section of barbecue used: open slats
   and flat plate

4 x 180g (6oz) slices yellow fin tuna

3 tablespoons extra virgin olive oil

ground black pepper

8–12 small Désirée potatoes

1 large red pepper

medium-sized plastic bag

250ml (8fl oz) Home-made Mayonnaise (see
   recipe page 128)

30ml (1fl oz) gin

salt and white pepper, to taste

oil spray

reserved extra virgin olive oil

IN THE KITCHEN

Trim the tuna if necessary, place in a bowl and drizzle over extra virgin olive oil. Sprinkle with a little ground black pepper.

Cover the potatoes with water, bring to the boil and simmer for 5 minutes or until just tender. Drain and set aside.

Cut the red pepper into large sections and cook on the barbecue.

When the pepper has cooled, remove it from the plastic bag and, under running water, lift and peel the skin away from the flesh. Drain and then put into a food processor. Add the mayonnaise, gin, salt and pepper to taste. Process until well combined.

AT THE BARBECUE

Spray the red pepper sections with oil and place them skin-side down on the open slats. Cook until the skins start to blister and turn black, then turn them and leave to cook for 2 minutes. Remove them from the barbecue and place them in a plastic bag, seal it and let cool for 10 minutes.

Spray the flat plate well with oil. Add all the potatoes, turning them after two minutes and then flatten or smash them with the back of a spatula. Pour on a little of the reserved extra virgin olive oil and turn potatoes as often as necessary to get them brown and crispy. Sprinkle with salt, pepper and oil as you go.

Cook the tuna when you have everything ready to go; tuna only takes a minute to cook and must be eaten straight away.

Put the tuna onto the flat plate, ensuring it is well oiled as the fish sticks easily. Turn after 30 seconds or so. The length of time depends on the thickness of each piece but the fish is better served rare to medium.

AT THE TABLE

Place the browned potatoes in the middle of each plate and top with a piece of tuna. Spoon over some of the red pepper mayonnaise and serve immediately.

ORANGE-INFUSED WHOLE SEA TROUT AND ORIENTAL SALAD

Serves 4

Temperature: medium

Section of barbecue used: open slats

1–1^1/$_2$kg (2–3lb) whole sea trout
   (or similar fish), scaled

aluminium foil

olive oil spray

4 tablespoons finely grated orange rind

2 shallots, peeled and quartered

2 tablespoons mandarin vodka

20 Chinese chives

150ml (5fl oz) vegetable oil

^{1}/$_2$ teaspoon sesame oil

60ml (2fl oz) rice vinegar

^{1}/$_2$ teaspoon crushed Szechuan pepper

Chinese leaves or mixed salad leaves

IN THE KITCHEN

Wash the fish, making sure the cavity is clean, and wipe dry. Slash the sides of the fish three times to allow it to cook evenly. Put a double layer of foil on your work bench, shiny-side up, and spray well with oil. Sprinkle 2 tablespoons of the orange rind on the foil and lay the fish on top. Fill the fish cavity with the shallots, then sprinkle the remaining 2 tablespoons of rind on top. Bring the foil up slightly around the sides of the fish and sprinkle on the vodka. Fold the foil around the fish, making a tight parcel.

Peel the oranges and cut into rounds; cut the chives into 6cm (2in) lengths.

Make the dressing by whisking the oils and slowly adding the rice vinegar; add the pepper and whisk to combine.

AT THE BARBECUE

Put the fish parcel on the open slats, seam-side down, and cook for 8 minutes. Turn the fish over and allow to cook for another 8 minutes. Carefully open the parcel (watch for escaping steam) and insert a sharp knife to see if the fish is cooked through. If not, close the parcel and cook until done — another 2–3 minutes each side.

AT THE TABLE

Assemble the salad in the kitchen by putting the leaves into a serving bowl and topping with the orange slices and chopped chives. At the table, serve the dressing separately.

Lift the foil back from the fish gently and serve the cooked fish flesh from the bone using a fork and spoon.

with

wings

CHARGRILLED DUCK BREASTS AND CURRIED CHICKPEAS

Duck breast meat is simply the best; it is deep and rich and the skin crisps beautifully on the barbecue. The flavours of the duck go well with Curried Chickpeas — this is a dish in its own right that you can offer to vegetarian guests.

Serves 4
Temperature: high/medium
Section of barbecue used: open slats

4 x 250g (8oz) duck breasts
Curried Chickpeas (see recipe page 98)
2 tablespoons rice vinegar
$1/2$ tablespoon cooking salt
1 tablespoon Sumac

IN THE KITCHEN

Slash the skin side of the breasts to allow the fat to escape during cooking.

Have the Curried Chickpeas ready for reheating.

AT THE BARBECUE

Rub the vinegar into the skin side of the duck breasts. Lay them over the high-heat part of the open slats, skin-sides down, and leave there for 1–2 minutes. Watch the breasts carefully as flames can scorch the skin, rather than brown it. Sprinkle the flesh side of the breasts with a little salt and half the Sumac and turn over. Sprinkle the skin sides with the remaining salt and Sumac and leave to cook for 1 minute.

Turn the breasts back onto their skin sides and move to a part of the open slats where the temperature is medium. Leave to cook a further 2–3 minutes. Turn breasts over and cook on the flesh side until done, 5–7 minutes. By now, the skin should be crispy and browned. Remove from the barbecue when done and let rest for at least 10 minutes before slicing.

AT THE TABLE

Either heat the Curried Chickpeas in the microwave or in a saucepan on the hob.

Cut the duck breasts on the diagonal. Place the chickpeas in the centre of a serving plate or bowl, top with the slices of duck and serve.

'CARPETBAG' CHICKEN BREASTS

Serves 4

Temperature: medium

Section of barbecue used: flat plate

4 medium-sized boneless chicken breasts

12–16 oysters, removed from the shell

4–8 slices Japanese pink pickled ginger

black pepper

4–8 slices Black Forest ham or Parma ham

cocktail sticks

olive oil spray

mixed seasonal vegetables, to serve

IN THE KITCHEN

Butterfly the chicken breasts: lay each one flat on a cutting board, slice almost through it and lift out one side to make the rough shape of a butterfly. Lay 3–4 oysters down the centre of each breast and top with slices of pickled ginger. Sprinkle on black pepper to taste. Fold the chicken meat around the oysters to form a neat parcel.

Wrap the breasts in slices of ham, and pin into place with cocktail sticks. Refrigerate until ready to use.

AT THE BARBECUE

Spray the plate with oil and add the chicken breasts. Seal on both sides for 2 minutes each side, then cover with a wok lid or stainless steel bowl. Cook until done, turning every now and then, for around 10 minutes, depending on the thickness of the breasts.

AT THE TABLE

Before serving, remove cocktail sticks and cut each breast in half on the diagonal. Serve with mixed seasonal vegetables.

CHICKEN BASTED WITH AUSTRALIAN NATIVE SPICES

Australian Native spices are used internationally and can be obtained from several producers in Australia. One such spice merchant is Ian Hemphill, who can mail spices around the world. Contact him through the web site www.herbies.com.au

Serves 4
Temperature: medium
Section of barbecue used: flat plate

2 x 1kg (2lb) chickens
4 teaspoons Australian Native
   BBQ mix (spices)
6 tablespoons vegetable oil
1 tablespoon lemon juice
sea salt, to taste
green salad or cooked seasonal vegetables,
   to serve

IN THE KITCHEN

Cut the chickens in half lengthwise down their middles. Make deep cuts in the skin sides of each half to allow for quicker cooking.

Mix the spices with the oil, lemon juice and salt. Using a pastry brush, baste the skin side of each chicken half with the oil mixture. Place chicken halves in a bowl for 20 minutes to marinate.

AT THE BARBECUE

Cook chicken halves on the barbecue, cut-sides down, for 5 minutes. Cover with a wok lid or stainless steel bowl.

Baste the skin sides of the chicken and turn over. Cook for 15 minutes, covered, ensuring the chicken does not stick or brown too quickly. Turn the chicken halves over and cook for a further 10 minutes on the cut sides. Baste the uppermost sides of the chicken, the skin sides, and turn to cook for 5 more minutes.

AT THE TABLE

Place chicken halves on platter and serve with dressed green salad or cooked seasonal vegetables of your choice.

CHICKEN AND BARBECUED CORN SALSA

Serves 4

Temperature: medium

Section of barbecue used: open slats

4 medium-sized boneless chicken breasts

1 large cob corn, husk and silk removed

125g (3^1/$_2$oz) tomatoes, unpeeled, cooked
    and diced

125g (3^1/$_2$oz) mango flesh, diced

1 very small red onion, peeled and
    finely diced

1 small banana chilli or other mild chilli,
    deseeded and very finely chopped

1 tablespoon parsley, chopped

salt and ground black pepper, to taste

2 tablespoons sherry vinegar

3 tablespoons olive oil

olive oil spray

20 asparagus tips

IN THE KITCHEN

Slice each chicken breast, on the diagonal, into 3 evenly-sized slices and flatten slightly.

When the cooked corn cob (see below) is cool enough to handle, cut the kernels from the cob into a bowl. Add the tomatoes, mango, onion, chilli, parsley, salt and pepper. Stir in the vinegar and oil.

AT THE BARBECUE

Spray the corn cob with oil and cook on the open slats, turning regularly to lightly brown the corn. When done, return it to the kitchen to become part of the salsa.

Put the asparagus tips onto the barbecue and lightly cook.

Spray the sliced chicken well with the oil. Place slices on the flat plate, turning to seal both sides. Transfer chicken to the open slats to cook through for approximately 2–3 minutes on each side.

AT THE TABLE

Spoon equal amounts of salsa onto each guest's plate and top with three chicken slices. Place asparagus tips on top of the chicken and serve.

CHICKEN PATTY AND SOURDOUGH SANDWICH

Chicken has always been really versatile. So many different types of bread are now available that deciding which one to use for a chicken sandwich is quite hard. Sourdough rye has marvellous flavours that make this sandwich a delicious meal for lunch.

Serves 4

Temperature: medium/high

Section of barbecue used:

   flat plate/open slats

500g (1lb) chicken mince

1 egg

1 carrot, peeled and finely grated

finely grated rind of 1 medium orange

1 tablespoon finely chopped fresh marjoram

sea salt and white pepper

2 medium-sized dried shiitake mushrooms, soaked in warm water to cover for 30–60 minutes (depending on size)

30–60g (1–2oz) fresh breadcrumbs

olive oil spray

8 slices sourdough rye bread

125ml (4fl oz) Home-made Mayonnaise (see recipe page 128)

60g (1³/₄oz) semi-roasted tomatoes, very finely chopped

mixed salad leaves

white balsamic vinegar, to dress the salad

IN THE KITCHEN

Place the chicken mince in a mixing bowl. Break the egg into it and add the carrot, orange rind, marjoram, salt and pepper. Remove the stems from the rehydrated mushrooms, chop finely and add them to the chicken mixture (keep the mushroom soaking liquid for use in soups or stocks). Mix the ingredients together and add enough breadcrumbs to absorb any excess liquid. The mixture will come away from your hands easily when it is ready.

Shape mixture into 4 evenly sized patties and refrigerate for 1 hour before cooking. (You can prepare the patties the day before, if you prefer.)

AT THE BARBECUE

Spray the flat plate with oil, then put on the chicken patties. Cook until done, turning the patties regularly. When the juices from each patty run clear, the meat is cooked.

Spray the rye bread with oil and toast each side on the open slats.

AT THE TABLE

Spread each slice of toasted bread with mayonnaise. Sprinkle some chopped semi-roasted tomatoes on four slices and top each one with a patty and another slice of toasted bread. Cut on the diagonal. Serve sandwiches on individual plates accompanied with dressed salad leaves.

DUCK SAUSAGES WITH ORANGE AND PARSNIP COMPOTE

Serves 4

Temperature: medium

Section of barbecue used: open slats and flat plate

4–8 duck sausages

400g (14oz) parsnip flesh, peeled, quartered and core removed

200g (7oz) broad beans

1 small salad onion, peeled

125ml (4fl oz) orange juice

2 tablespoons orange marmalade

olive oil spray

1 teaspoon truffle-infused oil

sea salt and white pepper to taste

2 tablespoons chopped chives

steamed green beans, to serve

IN THE KITCHEN

Separate the sausages if still linked.

Cut the parsnip into bite-sized pieces and blanch for 2 minutes; drain. Blanch the beans and peel their skins; the pods have brilliantly green flesh.

Slice the onion into fine rings.

To make the orange dressing, heat the orange juice and marmalade over low heat. Remove from heat when the marmalade is melted.

AT THE BARBECUE

Spray the flat plate well with oil and tip the parsnip pieces onto it. Cook quickly; this lovely root vegetable browns very quickly and should be only lightly browned. Place parsnips in a bowl. Add the onion slices, orange dressing and truffle-infused oil, and season with salt and pepper. Toss together and allow to cool. When cool, add the broad beans and chives, and combine well.

Cook the duck sausages on the flat plate, turning regularly until very firm to the touch with tongs; then transfer to the open slats and cook until crisp (about 1 minute each side).

AT THE TABLE

Serve the parsnip compôte in the centre of a platter and arrange the sausages around it. A small platter of buttered steamed green beans sets this dish off nicely.

DUCK QUESADILLAS

Serves 4

Temperature: medium high

Section of barbecue used: open slats
   and flat plate

750g (1^1/$_2$lb) boneless duck breasts
^{1}/$_4$ cup (^{3}/$_4$oz) jalapeño chillies, sliced
90g (3oz) onion, finely chopped
3 tablespoons coriander leaves, rinsed
salt and pepper, to taste
8 medium-sized flour tortillas
125g (4oz) Cheddar cheese, grated
olive oil spray
Semi-roasted Tomato Salsa
   (see recipe page 133)

IN THE KITCHEN

Trim the duck breasts of as much fat as possible.

Mix the chillies, onion, coriander leaves, salt and
pepper together.

Make the salsa.

AT THE BARBECUE

Put duck breasts on the open slats on medium-high, skin-side
down. Allow duck to brown very well, about 2 minutes, then
turn and cook for 5–7 minutes. Turn duck again and cook on
the skin side for 2 minutes. Remove and let rest for 5 minutes.
When cool enough to handle, slice duck into very thin strips.

To make quesadillas, lay a flour tortilla out flat and spoon a
quarter of the cheese over half of it. Add some duck slices and
then some of the chilli mix. Fold tortilla over the stuffing, tuck
the edge in under the filling and set aside. Repeat until all
tortillas are filled.

Spray the flat plate with oil and add the quesadillas,
folded-side up, and allow to cook for 1–2 minutes. Spray the
quesadilla with oil and flip it over quickly, holding the top as
you do to stop the filling from falling out. The cheese should
have melted enough to grip most of the filling.

Cook quesadillas for about 2 minutes on the second side
and lift off the plate when done.

AT THE TABLE

Serve the quesadillas on a large platter in the centre of the
table, with the salsa on the side.

QUAIL ON PINEAPPLE-SCENTED COUSCOUS

Serves 4
Temperature: medium
Section of barbecue used: open slats

4 large quail
60ml (2fl oz) olive oil plus 1 tablespoon
    extra
4 x 2cm ($^3/_4$in) thick slices fresh pineapple
1 small red onion, peeled
250g (9oz) dried couscous
500ml (1 pint) boiling water
3 tablespoons basil leaves
3 tablespoons mint leaves
1 teaspoon Baharat spice mix
sea salt and powdered black pepper
2 tablespoons toasted sesame seeds

IN THE KITCHEN

Cut the quail into quarters. Remove the winglets and place the quarters in a bowl; drizzle over 60ml (2fl oz) of olive oil, toss to coat the quail and refrigerate until ready for use.

Cut the pineapple slices into half moons and remove the core.

Finely dice the onion.

Put the couscous in a bowl and pour over boiling water. Leave for 30 seconds then add the diced onion and the tablespoon of olive oil; fork these through to stop the grains sticking together.

Cut the browned pineapple slices (see below) into small wedges and mix with the basil and mint leaves. Add the Baharat spice mix, salt and pepper and toss to combine the flavours. Allow to sit for a minute, then add to the couscous and fold in to meld the flavours.

AT THE BARBECUE

Remove the quail from the refrigerator 10 minutes before use and drain off the oil. Place on the barbecue, turn regularly and cook until done (about 2–3 minutes on each side). Remove when done and keep warm; quail tends to dry out when it is over-cooked. Sprinkle over the sesame seeds and toss to coat the quail pieces.

Flash-cook the pineapple slices by placing them on the open slats and turning them often until the slices brown slightly. When done, remove and return them to the kitchen.

AT THE TABLE

Place the couscous mixture on a large platter, arrange the pieces of quail on top and serve.

red

BARBECUED PORK AND GREEN APPLE SALAD 70

BARBECUED SIRLOIN AND GREEN CURRY DRESSING 72

BEEF, ONION AND CHIVE PANCAKES 73

BEEF FAJITAS 74

CALF'S LIVER, SKEWERED ONIONS AND CASHEW AND MUSTARD BUTTER 76

CARAWAY PORK CUTLETS, BASIL AND TOMATO SLAW 77

LAMB CUTLETS SALTIMBOCCA WITH PEA AND TOMATO LINGUINE 78

PEPPER-CRUSTED LAMB STEAKS WITH LENTIL, PEA AND MINT SALAD 80

PORK CHOPS AND SWEETCORN POTATO CAKES WITH BLUE
  CHEESE MAYONNAISE 83

VEAL CUTLETS WITH OLIVE, PARSLEY AND LIME PESTO 84

THE PERFECT BARBECUED STEAK 86

meat

BARBECUED PORK AND GREEN APPLE SALAD

Serves 4
Temperature: medium
**Section of barbecue used: flat plate
   and open slats**

400g (14oz) pork fillets

2 medium green apples or green mangoes

$^1/_2$ teaspoon salt

olive oil spray

3 cloves garlic, sliced

4 spring onions, trimmed and sliced
   diagonally

1 tablespoon Thai fish sauce (*nam pla*)

3 tablespoons roasted peanuts, crushed

1 teaspoon palm sugar

$^1/_2$ teaspoon ground white pepper

1 large green chilli, deseeded and
   finely sliced

IN THE KITCHEN

Trim the pork to make sure all fat and silver tissue is removed.

If using apples, core and quarter them, then slice very finely. If using mangoes, peel off the skin and slice the flesh from the stone, then cut very finely into batons.

Place the slices of fruit in a bowl, sprinkle with salt and toss.

AT THE BARBECUE

Spray the pork fillets with oil and put on the flat plate. Roll the fillets so they are sealed on all sides, then transfer to the open slats to cook through; be careful not to over-cook the pork. When cooked, remove to rest for 5 minutes before slicing.

Spray the flat plate with oil and toss on the garlic and spring onion slices for 1 minute, then remove and set aside.

AT THE TABLE

Slice the pork finely into 1–2cm ($^1/_2$–$^3/_4$ in) thick rounds and halve if large slices. Add pork slices to the apples (or mangoes) and add the other ingredients except for the chilli. Toss salad gently and then sprinkle the sliced chilli over the top.

BARBECUED SIRLOIN AND GREEN CURRY DRESSING

Serves 4

Temperature: very hot, then medium hot

**Section of barbecue used: flat plate
and open slats**

750g (1^1/$_2$lb) sirloin, in one piece with all
fat and connective tissue removed

125ml (4fl oz) coconut milk

125ml (4fl oz) Green Curry Paste (see recipe
page 127)

90g (2^1/$_2$oz) roasted peanuts, skins removed
and roughly chopped

500ml (1 pint) coconut cream

1 tablespoon demerara sugar, or palm sugar

2 teaspoons Thai fish sauce (*nam pla*)

3 long green chillies, deseeded and cut into
fine strips

3 Kaffir lime leaves, veins removed and cut
into fine strips

olive oil spray

fresh coriander leaves

cooked rice vermicelli noodles or steamed
fragrant rice, to serve

IN THE KITCHEN

Check that the sirloin is thoroughly trimmed.

Bring the coconut milk to the boil in a wok and cook for a minute or so. When the milk has separated, add the Green Curry Paste and stir for 2 minutes. The liquid will become very fragrant.

Add ^{2}/$_3$ of the peanuts and the coconut cream. Cook until heated through, then add the sugar and fish sauce and stir in. The liquid should now be heated, salty and sweet — adjust the flavours to your liking.

Add the chillies and Kaffir lime leaves, remove from the heat and stir for a minute.

AT THE BARBECUE

Spray the beef with oil, put onto a very hot flat plate and seal by cooking for a minute on all sides. Transfer onto medium-hot open slats and cook for 5–7 minutes on each side or until medium-rare — length of cooking time depends on the thickness of the beef. Remove and set aside in a warm place for 15 minutes.

AT THE TABLE

When the beef is ready, thinly slice and lay on a shallow platter. Pour the curry dressing over the beef, sprinkle on the remaining peanuts and tear the coriander leaves over the top. You can serve the beef with cooked rice vermicelli noodles or steamed Thai fragrant rice.

BEEF, ONION AND CHIVE PANCAKES

Serves 4
Temperature: medium
Section of barbecue used: flat plate

125g (4oz) self-raising flour

salt and white pepper, to taste

1 egg

250–300ml (8–10fl oz) beer, at room
   temperature

150g (5oz) diced beef, roasted or boiled

2 tablespoons whole-grain mustard

2 medium onions, finely diced

1 tablespoon chopped chives

olive oil spray

Barbecue Tomato Relish (see recipe page 122)

IN THE KITCHEN

Sift the flour, salt and white pepper into a bowl. Mix the egg with the beer and stir into the flour with a wooden spoon. Tip in the beef, mustard, onions and chives, stir well and leave to rest for 15 minutes.

AT THE BARBECUE

Spray the flat plate well. Make the pancakes by dropping the meat batter onto the flat plate. Do as many as you like at one time, but ensure you leave enough room to flip the pancakes (I normally do no more than 4 at a time).

The size of the pancakes can be varied — a dessertspoon of batter produces a good medium-sized pancake while a tablespoon makes a large one that is enough for one person. However, once you start eating these with the Barbecue Tomato Relish, it's hard to stop! Smaller pancakes are great to pass around at the barbecue.

Whichever size pancake you decide on, continue until all the batter is used.

AT THE TABLE

These pancakes are excellent served at the table with a good salad. Serve the Barbecue Tomato Relish on the side.

BEEF FAJITAS

Serves 4
Temperature: very hot
Section of barbecue used: flat plate
   and open slats

500g (1lb) rump steak
2 tablespoons of light olive oil
2 tablespoons red wine vinegar
$^1/_2$ tablespoon ground allspice
$^1/_2$ tablespoon dried oregano
2 tablespoons dried onion flakes
1 teaspoon salt
$^1/_4$ teaspoon chilli powder
8 wheat flour tortillas
olive oil spray
60g (2oz) lettuce, shredded
60g (2$^1/_4$oz) carrot, grated
2 medium-sized salad tomatoes, cut into
   wedges
125ml (4oz) sour cream

IN THE KITCHEN

Cut the steak across the grain into strips 1cm (½in) wide and place in bowl.

Mix together the oil, vinegar, allspice, oregano, onion flakes, salt, and chilli powder, and pour over the steak strips. Stir so all pieces are coated, cover and refrigerate for at least 2 hours.

AT THE BARBECUE

Tip the strips onto the flat plate and spread them out over it. Cook steak by tossing and lifting the strips and allowing them to brown. The steak will cook in 5–6 minutes; remove when done.

Spray the tortillas with oil and heat very quickly on the open slats for 30 seconds each side. Remove them and keep them warm.

AT THE TABLE

Serve the steak strips on a platter in the centre of the table, surrounded by the lettuce, carrots, tomatoes, tortillas and sour cream on separate platters.

Assemble the fajitas by placing some lettuce on each tortilla, then some carrot and steak strips, topped with sour cream. Add some tomato wedges. To eat, roll up the fajitas or fold them, whichever is easier.

CALF'S LIVER, SKEWERED ONIONS AND CASHEW AND MUSTARD BUTTER

Serves 4

Temperature: medium

Section of barbecue used: flat plate and open slats

500g (1lb) calf's liver, cut into slices
1cm ($^1/_2$ in) thick

4 small onions, peeled and cut into rounds
1cm ($^1/_2$ in) thick

4 stainless steel skewers

8 small potatoes, cut into halves

olive oil spray

sea salt

$^1/_2$ tablespoon smoked paprika

Mustard and Cashew Nut Butter
(see recipe page 120)

IN THE KITCHEN

Ensure all skin is removed from the outside of each slice of liver.

Thread the onion slices onto the skewers laid flat on the work surface (I am able to get 3 slices out of each onion).

Boil the potato halves in salted water for 4–5 minutes, then drain.

AT THE BARBECUE

Spray the flat plate with oil and put the skewered onions on. Spray the potatoes with oil and put them on the open slats. Sprinkle onions and potatoes with salt and turn frequently to cook.

Spray the liver with oil and put onto the flat plate, sprinkle with a little smoked paprika and salt, and cook for 1 minute. Turn the liver slices and repeat on the other side. Liver cooks quickly and it is important to serve it medium; liver becomes dry and rubbery if cooked to well done.

AT THE TABLE

Place 4 potato pieces in the centre of each plate and top with 1–2 slices of liver. Arrange the onion rings beside the liver and potatoes and top the liver with a couple of slices of Mustard and Cashew Nut Butter. Serve as the butter starts to melt over the liver.

CARAWAY PORK CUTLETS, BASIL AND TOMATO SLAW

Serves 4

Temperature: medium

Section of barbecue used: flat plate
and open slats

4–8 pork cutlets, depending on size

1 teaspoon caraway seeds

250ml (8fl oz) beer

1 small onion, finely diced

2–3 bay leaves

125g (4oz) Savoy cabbage, finely shredded

large handful basil leaves, roughly torn

2 large ripe tomatoes, cut into wedges

1 small salad onion

60ml (2fl oz) verjuice

2 tablespoons olive oil

2 rashers bacon

sea salt, to taste

IN THE KITCHEN

Trim excess fat from the pork and place in a glass bowl. Add the caraway seeds, beer, small diced onion and the bay leaves. Move the cutlets around, and then let them soak in the beer for 10 minutes.

Remove the rind from the bacon rashers and cut into fine strips ½cm (¼in) thick.

Put the cabbage in a bowl, and add the basil leaves and tomatoes. Slice the salad onion into rings and put in with the other slaw ingredients. Pour in the verjuice, olive oil and cooked bacon pieces (see below), add salt and tumble to combine.

AT THE BARBECUE

Place the strips of bacon on the flat plate, and move them around while they cook until they become crispy. When the bacon is done, transfer to a plate lined with kitchen paper to cool.

Place the cutlets on the flat plate where the bacon was cooked, and cook on each side for 2 minutes until the meat is sealed. Then spoon a little of the beer and caraway seed mixture onto the pork while it continues to cook.

To finish the cutlets, flash-cook them on both sides on the open slats, then remove from the barbecue.

AT THE TABLE

Serve the pork by spooning some slaw into the centre of each plate and arranging the pork cutlet/s on top.

LAMB CUTLETS SALTIMBOCCA WITH PEA AND TOMATO LINGUINE

Serves 4

Temperature: medium

Section of barbecue used: flat plate

8–12 trimmed lamb cutlets, depending
   on size and appetite

8–12 large sage leaves

8–12 thin slivers Parmesan cheese

8–12 slices Parma ham

2 tablespoons olive oil

500g (1lb) cooked and oiled linguine

120g (4oz) peas, fresh or frozen

2 medium-sized ripe tomatoes, diced

2 tablespoons tomato sauce for pasta

60ml (2fl oz) lamb or beef stock

sea salt and ground black pepper

IN THE KITCHEN

On top of each cutlet, place a sage leaf, then enough Parmesan cheese to cover both sage and cutlet. Wrap in a slice of Parma ham and set aside. Repeat with the remaining cutlets.

Just before the lamb is ready to come off the barbecue (see below), heat olive oil in a suitable pan over medium heat. Add the linguine, peas, tomatoes and tomato sauce. Stir, then pour in the stock so that the peas and tomatoes cook and provide a good sauce for the linguine. Season with salt and pepper.

AT THE BARBECUE

Cook the lamb cutlets on the flat plate, turning regularly. When the cheese starts to seep through the crisped Parma ham, the cutlets are ready. Immediately transfer the cutlets to a platter.

AT THE TABLE

Serve the cutlets on a platter and the linguine in a large bowl. A garden salad goes well with this dish.

PEPPER-CRUSTED LAMB STEAKS WITH LENTIL, PEA AND MINT SALAD

Crusting meats in cracked pepper is a longstanding technique that was particularly popular in the early 1970s. This dish, like a lot of retro dishes, is being revitalised and served once again to a completely new audience.

Serves 4

Temperature: medium

Section of barbecue used: flat plate and open slats

4 lamb steaks

cracked black pepper

200g (7oz) dried green lentils

1 large onion, roughly chopped

200g (7oz) sugar snap peas

200g (7oz) peas

2 eggs, for omelettes

2 tablespoons finely chopped parsley

olive oil spray

3 tbsp mint leaves, torn

125ml (4fl oz) olive oil

60ml (2fl oz) lemon juice

sea salt, to taste

4 lemon wedges

IN THE KITCHEN

Trim the steaks of all fat and roll them in as much or as little cracked black pepper as you like. Refrigerate until ready to use.

Soak the lentils in cold water for 20 minutes. Drain and put into a saucepan with the onion. Cover well with water, bring to the boil, then reduce to a simmer and cook until the lentils are soft but not falling apart — about 30–40 minutes. Drain and rinse the lentils under cold water.

Blanch the sugar snap peas and the peas.

Make a 1-egg omelette by beating 1 egg with 1 tablespoon of water and 1 tablespoon of parsley. Pour the mixture into a well-oiled, non-stick small omelette pan and let it run all over the base of the pan. The omelette should be very thin and resemble a thin pancake. When set and lightly browned, flip over, leave for 15 seconds then slide out of the pan onto a chopping board. Repeat for the other omelette. When both omelettes are cooked and cooled, roll them into a sausage shape and cut into strips ½cm (¼in) wide.

Assemble the salad by combining the lentils and onion, the two lots of peas, the sliced omelettes (open the strips out so they look like cooked fettucine) and the mint. Toss with the oil, lemon juice and salt.

AT THE BARBECUE

Spray the flat plate well with oil and put the lamb steaks on. Cook for 2 minutes on each side to seal them, then cover with a wok lid or stainless steel bowl. Cook for up to 4–5 minutes on each side (depending on the size of each steak), then remove and let rest for 10 minutes before slicing.

Place the lemon wedges on the open slats cut-side down for 1 minute before serving the lamb.

AT THE TABLE

Serve the lamb on individual plates. Slice each steak into 4 equal slices (refer to the note below) and place on the plate with a lemon wedge to one side. Place the bowl of lentil salad in the middle of the table.

NOTE: The size of the lamb steaks varies according to where you obtain them. Adjust the cooking time for the lamb to suit the size of steak you have bought.

PORK CHOPS AND SWEETCORN POTATO CAKES WITH BLUE CHEESE MAYONNAISE

Serves 4

Temperature: medium

Section of barbecue used: open slats and flat plate

4–8 pork chops, depending on size

250ml (8fl oz) Home-made Mayonnaise (see recipe page 128)

120g (4oz) blue cheese of your choice, crumbled

1 tablespoon white wine vinegar

1 tablespoon finely chopped spring onion

400g (14oz) mashed potatoes, at room temperature

4 tablespoons tinned sweetcorn, drained

1 egg, beaten

salt and white pepper, to taste

dried breadcrumbs

olive oil

steamed green vegetables, to serve

IN THE KITCHEN

Trim the pork chops of their rind, if you prefer. Set to one side. Put the mayonnaise and cheese into a bowl and whisk in the vinegar until combined. Stir in the spring onion.

Make the potato cakes by mixing the potatoes, sweetcorn, egg and salt and pepper together; add enough breadcrumbs to take up the moisture and to make a firm mixture. Evenly divide the potato mixture and shape into 4 patties. Refrigerate patties if not using immediately.

AT THE BARBECUE

Barbecue the chops until done. Start cooking them on the open slats and then transfer to the flat plate if chops are very thick. Check that they are cooked by inserting a sharp knife into the chops — when juices run clear, they are ready to serve.

Pour oil onto the flat plate and cook the potato cakes until lightly browned on each side.

AT THE TABLE

Serve the potato cakes with the pork chops, with the blue cheese mayonnaise on the side. Freshly steamed green vegetables really complete this meal.

VEAL CUTLETS WITH OLIVE, PARSLEY AND LIME PESTO

Serves 4

Temperature: hot then medium heat

Section of barbecue used: open slats

4 x 200g (7oz) veal cutlets

OLIVE, PARSLEY AND LIME PESTO

20 green olives, stoned

grated rind of 2 limes

juice of 1 lime

2 cloves garlic, peeled and halved

1 tablespoon pine nuts

45g (1$^{1}/_{2}$oz) flat-leaf parsley

90ml (2$^{1}/_{2}$fl oz) extra virgin olive oil

400g (14oz) waxy potatoes

olive oil spray

chopped fresh oregano, to taste

sea salt and ground black pepper

IN THE KITCHEN

Trim the veal cutlets if necessary, cover with clingfilm and refrigerate until ready to use.

Put the olives, lime rind, lime juice, garlic, pine nuts and parsley in a food processor bowl and start the motor. Gradually pour in the olive oil and work until combined. The mixture should be roughly chopped when you remove it from the processor bowl; cover and refrigerate.

Wash potatoes and peel, if desired; if potatoes are large, cut into halves or quarters. Boil potatoes for 3 minutes, then drain and cool. Refrigerate until ready to use.

Remove veal and potatoes from the refrigerator 15 minutes before use to bring them to room temperature.

AT THE BARBECUE

Spray the cutlets with plenty of oil and place on hot barbecue. Leave for a minute to seal, then turn and seal the other side for a minute. Move cutlets to medium heat and cook them to your liking. Sprinkle on some oregano and press into each cutlet with the back of the cooking spatula. Turn cutlets only one more time and repeat the oregano on the other side. Sprinkle with salt and pepper on the second turning only — do not put on raw meat.

Spray the potatoes well and put on to medium heat. Sprinkle with salt and pepper and turn regularly until browned, crisp and cooked through.

AT THE TABLE

Transfer veal cutlets from the barbecue to a plate and let them rest for 3 minutes. Place equal quantities of potato in the centre of each plate and top with the veal cutlets. Spoon some of the pesto over the cutlets and put the remainder on the table.

THE PERFECT BARBECUED STEAK

Choosing the correct beef cut is really crucial to the finished product. Cook your steak this way and never serve it cooked any more than medium. This was my recommendation in *Barbecued!* and nothing has changed! I have had so many comments about this recipe that it simply had to be repeated. This time I am suggesting some good butters to be served on top ... let them ooze all over the steak.

Serves 4
Temperature: high and medium
**Section of barbecue used: flat plate
and open slats**

4 sirloin steaks 4cm (1^1/$_2$ in) thick,
   well marbled
olive oil spray
salt and ground black pepper

IN THE KITCHEN

Trim as much fat from your steaks as you like but ensure that at least ^{1}/$_2$ cm (¼ in) is left.

AT THE BARBECUE

Spray the steaks with oil and place on a high flat plate. Leave the meat for 2 minutes without disturbing it. Do not at any time puncture the steaks with forks or knives, as by doing this you release the vital juices of the meat.

Spray the steaks lightly with oil and turn onto another part of the high flat plate. It is best not to turn the steak and replace it on the same spot as the intensity of heat is gone. Cook a further 2 minutes.

Flip the steaks again but this time transfer onto the open slats. Cook for 2 minutes each side sprinkling with salt and pepper as you turn them.

Lift steaks onto a plate and allow to rest for 5 minutes before serving.

AT THE TABLE

Place the steaks on individual plates with the vegetables or salads of your choice, and serve with your favourite flavoured butters (see recipes pages 120–121).

You will have noticed that I recommend leaving some fat on the steak; this is essential to maximise flavour. If you prefer your steak without the fat, slice it off after it has been cooked. Marbled beef is identified by the streaks of white fat that are visible in the red meat. These thin lines of fat melt in the cooking process and give that superb flavour to barbecued beef steak.

on the

side

BABY LEEKS WITH OREGANO DRESSING

Serves 4
Temperature: medium
Section of barbecue used: open slats

16 baby leeks

OREGANO DRESSING
1 shallot, peeled and very finely chopped
2 tablespoons sherry vinegar
2 tablespoons walnut oil
1 tablespoon roughly chopped oregano
white pepper

olive oil spray
sea salt
2 tomatoes, flesh only, and julienned
oregano sprigs for garnish

IN THE KITCHEN

Trim the leeks to around 15cm (6in) in length, removing all excess green parts. Peel off the outside layer of the leeks and ensure the root parts are trimmed. Whisk together the shallots, vinegar, oil and chopped oregano, adding pepper to taste, to make the dressing.

Place the leeks in the oregano dressing to marinate and allow to cool. Then cover and set aside for at least 2 hours. While it's preferable to have the leeks at room temperature, if you are not using them within 2 hours, store them in the refrigerator.

AT THE BARBECUE

Spray the leeks with oil and position them on the barbecue so they sit across the slats at right angles. Sprinkle with a little salt and cook until they soften; leeks lose their crispness if cooked right through. Test the leeks by inserting a skewer to check how firm they are in the centre. When cooked, remove the leeks and return to the kitchen.

AT THE TABLE

Place the leeks on individual plates; sprinkle over the julienned tomatoes and garnish with oregano sprigs. Spoon on any extra dressing.

BACON AND PEACH SALAD WITH BLUE CHEESE DRESSING

The arrival of peaches in shops and markets always signals the start of summer, and it's good to use them in as many ways as we can. In this salad, the saltiness of the bacon and the sweetness of the peaches are a perfect foil for the rich cheese dressing.

Serves 4
Temperature: medium
Section of barbecue used: flat plate

4 medium bacon rashers
2 peaches, just ripe
juice of 1 small lemon
mixed salad leaves
1 red pepper
1 small salad onion, peeled
100g (3 $^1/_2$ oz) creamy blue vein cheese
2 tablespoons white balsamic vinegar
ground black pepper, to taste

IN THE KITCHEN

Cut the rind from the bacon and then cut into 5cm (2in) lengths.

Halve the peaches, cut into 8 wedges and toss in the lemon juice.

Ensure lettuce leaves are crisp and refrigerated for use. Remove the seeds from the pepper and cut the flesh into strips.

Slice the onion very finely into rounds.

Mash the cheese with the vinegar — don't worry about the lumpy dressing that results.

AT THE BARBECUE

Cook the bacon on the flat plate until crisp, then toss on the peaches and lightly brown them, taking care not to over-cook. Remove both from the barbecue.

AT THE TABLE

Assemble the salad by placing the lettuce leaves, pepper and onion in layers in a salad bowl. Top with the peach wedges and bacon, then spoon over the cheese dressing and sprinkle with plenty of ground black pepper. Toss together and serve immediately.

BARBECUED HALLOUMI, COS, ASPARAGUS AND AVOCADO SALAD

Serves 4

Temperature: medium/hot

Section of barbecue used: flat plate and
open slats

8 slices halloumi cheese, 2cm ($^3/_4$in) thick

250g (8oz) cos lettuce, washed

2 spring onions

60ml (2fl oz) raspberry vinegar

2 tablespoons Home-made Mayonnaise
(see recipe page 128)

1 clove garlic, crushed

ground black pepper, to taste

olive oil spray

12 asparagus spears, trimmed to green
part only

1 avocado, peeled and sliced

IN THE KITCHEN

As halloumi can be salty, wash it well in water.

Cut Cos lettuce into bite-sized pieces and keep crisp
in refrigerator.

Cut the white part of the spring onions into pieces 3cm (1in)
long; shred the green tops very finely for garnish.

Make the dressing by whisking together the vinegar,
mayonnaise, garlic and pepper.

AT THE BARBECUE

Spray the flat plate well with oil and add the halloumi slices.
Cook quickly, letting them brown and crisp, then turn them
and do the same on the other side.

Cook the asparagus spears on the open slats, turning
regularly; they only need to be heated and must not lose
their crunchiness.

Remove halloumi and asparagus from the barbecue.

AT THE TABLE

Place the lettuce, avocado slices and onion pieces in a salad
bowl. Top with the warm asparagus and slices of halloumi,
then sprinkle over the green onion tops. Pour over the dressing
and serve immediately.

BARBECUED TURKISH BREAD

Serves 4

Temperature: medium

Section of barbecue used: flat plate and
open slats

4 individual sandwich-sized pieces of pide
(Turkish bread)

250ml (8fl oz) Home-made Mayonnaise (see
recipe page 128)

250ml (8fl oz) hummus

200g (7oz) mozzarella cheese, grated

2 medium-sized tomatoes, sliced into rounds

sea salt and ground black pepper

basil leaves

mixed salad leaves

olive oil spray

balsamic vinegar

olive oil

IN THE KITCHEN

Cut each piece of pide in half, to obtain a top and bottom half.

Mix together the mayonnaise and hummus, and spread it on the bottom pieces of bread. Top each piece with equal amounts of cheese and tomato, and add salt, pepper and basil leaves to taste. Spread the remaining mayo and hummus mixture on the top pieces of bread and place them gently on top of the assembled ingredients.

Ensure the salad leaves are crisp and refrigerated, ready to use.

AT THE BARBECUE

Spray the flat plate with oil and place on it each of the sandwiches. Leave to cook for 2 minutes, then turn quickly and press down with the spatula. Cook for another 2 minutes.

Turn each sandwich over gently. By now, the cheese should be melting and holding the ingredients in place. Gently slide the sandwiches over onto the open slats and cook until both sides are crisp.

AT THE TABLE

Transfer the sandwiches to the table, cut them into triangles and arrange on a platter. Dress the salad leaves with balsamic vinegar and oil, toss in a salad bowl and serve separately.

BARBECUED MUSHROOM, CARROT AND PECORINO ROMANO SALAD

Mushrooms add a special flavour when cooked, and in this recipe, they combine with other earthy ingredients to make a wonderful dish for summer lunches.

Serves 4

Temperature: high/medium

Section of barbecue used: open slats and flat plate

20 button mushrooms

4 medium-sized carrots

4 slices day-old white bread

125ml (4fl oz) olive oil

1 tablespoon finely chopped marjoram

2 tablespoons balsamic vinegar

sea salt and ground black pepper, to taste

olive oil spray

mixed salad leaves

200g (7oz) Pecorino Romano cheese, cubed or sliced

IN THE KITCHEN

Trim the mushrooms of excess stalk.

Trim the ends from the carrots and cut into halves lengthwise.

Remove the crusts from the bread and cut into cubes to make croutons.

Make the dressing by whisking the oil and marjoram together in a bowl. When combined, whisk in the vinegar with salt and pepper to taste, and set aside but do not refrigerate.

AT THE BARBECUE

Spray the mushrooms with oil and put on the open slats. Cook quickly, turning regularly and remove them when they are well-marked but firm.

Spray the carrots with oil and cook quickly on the open slats—remove when just done; the carrots should not lose their crunchiness.

Spray the bread cubes well with oil and put on the flat plate, turning regularly until browned and crisp. You may need to spray with oil as you turn to allow for even browning.

AT THE TABLE

Place the salad leaves in a large bowl, top with the warm mushrooms, carrots and cheese. Spoon the dressing over the salad, toss it, top with the croutons and serve immediately.

BARBECUED NECTARINE WEDGES, PANCETTA AND FETA SALAD

Over the years, the quality and size of nectarines has improved enormously and they can withstand processing without bruising. For this dish, select fruit that is just ripe so you get the benefit of the full flavour.

Serves 4
Temperature: high/medium
Section of barbecue used: open slats and flat plate

2 large nectarines, just ripe
125ml (4fl oz) vanilla olive oil
1 teaspoon Dijon mustard
2 tablespoons white wine vinegar
olive oil spray
8–12 slices pancetta
4 x 2cm ($3/4$in) slices Cinnamon Courgette Bread (see recipe page 125)
mixed salad leaves
200g (7oz) feta cheese, crumbled

IN THE KITCHEN

Wash the nectarines and halve, then cut the halves into wedges.

Make the dressing by whisking together the oil and mustard; when combined, whisk in the vinegar. Set aside but do not refrigerate.

AT THE BARBECUE

Spray the nectarine wedges with oil and place on the open slats. Cook the nectarine wedges quickly, turning them regularly and remove when they are well marked.

At the same time, cook the pancetta on the flat plate. When crisped and browned, remove to a plate lined with kitchen paper.

Spray the bread with oil and brown both sides on the open slats.

AT THE TABLE

Place the salad leaves in a large bowl, top with the nectarine wedges and feta cheese, crumble over the crispy pancetta and add the dressing. Serve the Cinnamon Courgette Bread separately.

CURRIED CHICKPEAS

I have enjoyed many Indian meals in London with a great foodie friend, Clare Ferguson, who writes cookbooks and does some amazing food styling. This is an adaptation of her recipe for curried chickpeas.

Serves 4

400g (14oz) pre-cooked chickpeas, drained
1 teaspoon coriander seeds, roasted
6 green cardamom pods, broken open
5cm (2in) cinnamon stick, in pieces
7 whole cloves
1 teaspoon white peppercorns
1 teaspoon poppy seeds
5cm (2in) piece root ginger, peeled and
   chopped
4 cloves garlic, chopped
1 small onion, chopped
2 tablespoons peanut oil or ghee
1 tablespoon black mustard seeds
salt (optional)
3–4 tablespoons whole mint leaves

IN THE KITCHEN

Wash the chickpeas and set aside.

Using a mortar and pestle, grind to a paste the coriander seeds, cardamom pods, cinnamon, cloves, white peppercorns, poppy seeds, ginger, garlic and onion.

Heat the oil in a saucepan to smoking point and add the black mustard seeds, then put the lid on the saucepan and cook for 30 seconds. Add the spice paste and chickpeas and cook for a further minute. Add enough water to completely cover the peas, reduce the heat and simmer with the lid on for 45 minutes. Check for seasoning and add salt if necessary.

AT THE TABLE

You can serve this stunning curry on its own with the mint leaves tumbled over it, or with meats of your choice.

FIELD MUSHROOMS WITH WASABI BUTTER

Serves 4
Temperature: medium
Section of barbecue used: open slats

4 large field mushrooms
3 tablespoons chopped parsley
3 tablespoons chopped spring onions
60ml (2fl oz) olive oil
olive oil spray
Wasabi Butter (see recipe page 121)

IN THE KITCHEN

Trim the field mushrooms of their stems to make their brown undersides as flat as possible.

Mix the parsley, onions and oil together.

AT THE BARBECUE

Spray the top of the mushrooms and put them on the barbecue with the brown, gill-sides up. Evenly distribute the parsley-oil mix over the mushrooms.

Cook the mushrooms for 2 minutes and then turn them over. Cook for a further 2 minutes and turn them over again for another minute.

AT THE TABLE

Place a field mushroom in the centre of individual serving plates and top with 1 or 2 slices of Wasabi Butter.

Field mushrooms vary in size and shape depending on how old they are. The older they get the thicker they become and the skin gets tough. If your field mushrooms are old, you may like to peel the skin off. However, this weakens the mushrooms' ability to remain whole while being cooked, so if you leave the skin on, you may have to cook them longer.

CELLOPHANE NOODLE SALAD

Cellophane noodles are also known as mung bean thread noodles and are made of mung bean and tapioca starch, which means they contain no traces of wheat and are thus ideal for people with a gluten intolerance.

Serves 4

125g (4oz) dried cellophane noodles

1 carrot, peeled and finely julienned

100g (3 $^1/_2$oz) daikon (Japanese white radish), peeled and finely julienned

$^1/_2$ Lebanese or ordinary small cucumber, cut lengthwise, deseeded and julienned

1 very small red onion, peeled and very finely sliced

40g (1$^1/_2$oz) Japanese pink pickled ginger, julienned

50g (2oz) mangetout, washed and crisp from the refrigerator

1 red pepper, finely julienned

3 tablespoons fresh coriander leaves

NOODLE SALAD DRESSING

1 tablespoon palm sugar

125ml (4fl oz) coconut cream

juice of 2 limes

1 tablespoon nam prik (see recipe page 131)

1–2 tablespoons Thai fish sauce (*nam pla*)

IN THE KITCHEN

Put the noodles into a large bowl and pour boiling water over to cover them. Set aside for 5–7 minutes and then strain noodles, running them under cold water to stop cooking. Ensure all the water is removed then transfer the noodles to a mixing bowl and allow to cool for 10 minutes.

Add all other ingredients except for the coriander leaves and dressing and toss gently using your hands.

Make the dressing by combining all the ingredients and mixing well. Pour over the assembled salad ingredients and toss gently, then top with the coriander leaves and serve.

LENTIL AND BEETROOT BURGERS

Serves 4

Temperature: medium

Section of barbecue used: open slats

4 lentil burgers (vegetarian burgers)

4 burger baps

olive oil spray

Spicy Black-Eyed Bean Paste

  (see recipe page 134)

lettuce leaves, crisp and shredded

4 slices red onion

4–8 slices beetroot

8 slices tomato

salt and ground black pepper, to taste

potato salad or coleslaw, to serve

IN THE KITCHEN

If the lentil burgers are frozen, thaw them out. Otherwise, bring them to room temperature at least 5 minutes before use.
  Cut the burger baps through the middle to obtain top and bottom halves.

AT THE BARBECUE

Spray the lentil burgers with oil, put on the barbecue and turn as they brown. Spray the halved rolls with oil and brown them on the barbecue.

AT THE TABLE

Spread Spicy Black-Eyed Bean Paste on each half of the burger rolls, then add shredded lettuce to the bottom halves, top with a slice of onion, 1 or 2 slices of beetroot and 2 slices of tomato and season to taste. Put the cooked lentil burger on top, press down firmly and cut in half, if preferred. You can serve the burgers with potato salad or coleslaw.

PUMPKIN, KUMERA AND TOFU SALAD WITH BLOOD ORANGE DRESSING

Serves 4

Temperature: medium

Section of barbecue used: flat plate and open slats

300g (10oz) Japanese pumpkin (or butternut squash), skin on and cut into bite-sized pieces

300g (10oz) kumera (orange sweet potato), cut into bite-sized pieces

250ml (8fl oz) olive oil

200g (7oz) tofu

BLOOD ORANGE DRESSING

3 blood oranges, cut into quarters

250ml (4fl oz) olive oil

$^1/_2$ teaspoon Sumac

$^1/_2$ teaspoon honey

sea salt and ground black pepper, to taste

1 tablespoon Nigella seeds (or toasted sesame seeds)

IN THE KITCHEN

Place the pumpkin and kumera in a bowl and pour over 125ml (4fl oz) oil to coat well, retaining the rest of the oil for the tofu.

Carefully cut the tofu into bite-sized pieces, around 4cm long by 2cm thick (1½in by ¾in).

To make the dressing, squeeze the juice from the barbecued orange quarters (see below) into a bowl, removing any pips. Add the oil, Sumac, honey, salt and pepper and combine well with a whisk.

AT THE BARBECUE

Put the orange quarters over the open slats for about 1 minute or until marked; remove orange quarters and return them to the kitchen to cool.

Place the pumpkin and kumera on the flat plate. Make sure the pieces are sitting flat then cover with a wok lid or a stainless steel bowl; turn regularly. When cooked through, remove from barbecue and drain well on kitchen paper.

Put the reserved 125ml (4fl oz) oil onto the flat plate and carefully place the tofu pieces on it, turning gently to brown and crisp them. Remove and drain on kitchen paper.

AT THE TABLE

Place the pumpkin and kumera on a flat platter, top with the tofu, spoon over the dressing and sprinkle with the Nigella seeds (or toasted sesame seeds).

SPICY AUBERGINE AND DAL ON CHAPATTIS

Serves 4

Temperature: medium/high

Section of barbecue used: flat plate and open slats

2 medium-sized aubergines, 500g (1lb) total weight

1 small onion

1 teaspoon black mustard seeds

1 teaspoon garam masala

$1/2$ teaspoon chilli powder

2 medium-sized green chillies, roughly chopped

4 tablespoons vegetable oil

2 medium tomatoes

Dal (Lentil Purée) (see recipe page 129)

olive oil spray

4 large chapattis

250ml (8fl oz) plain yoghurt

mint leaves, torn

IN THE KITCHEN

Trim the aubergines and then cut into 2cm (¾in) cubes. Peel and roughly dice the onion and combine in a bowl with the aubergine cubes.

Crush the mustard seeds using a mortar and pestle or in a food processor. Add the garam masala, chilli powder and chillies, and pound really well. When combined, pour in the oil and mix well. Pour the chilli mixture over the aubergine and onions, toss well and set aside for 10 minutes.

Dice the tomatoes.

Make the Dal.

AT THE BARBECUE

Spray the flat plate well with oil and place the aubergine mixture on it. Keep lifting and tossing the mixture while it cooks; when done, remove and keep warm.

Spray the chapattis with oil, place on the open slats and heat through. Flip chapattis over a couple of times to keep them pliable, and remove when lightly browned.

AT THE TABLE

Place the cooked aubergine in a suitable bowl with the chapattis, Dal, diced tomatoes, yoghurt and mint leaves. Let guests assemble their own chapattis by spreading Dal on each chapatti, piling some of the spicy aubergine down the middle of it, and adding tomato, yoghurt and mint leaves. Roll up and eat!

STAR ANISE-SCENTED BEETROOT, GOAT'S CHEESE AND GRAPEFRUIT SALAD

Serves 4

Temperature: low to medium

Section of barbecue used: open slats

3 beetroot, about the size of tennis balls

olive oil spray

aluminium foil

9 whole star anise

2 medium pink grapefruit

mixed salad leaves, washed and crisp
   in the refrigerator

200g (7oz) soft goat's cheese

90ml (2^1/$_2$fl oz) olive oil

sea salt

croutons

IN THE KITCHEN

Trim and wash the beetroot and then dry. Loosely wrap the beetroot and 3 whole star anise in a sheet of foil sprayed with oil, with the shiny side of the foil inside so as not to reflect the heat during cooking.

Peel the grapefruit and cut the membrane away from the segments; do this over a bowl so you collect the juices as they run from the grapefruit. Refrigerate the segments and squeeze the membranes of their juices into the retained juices.

When the beetroot is cooked (see below) allow it to rest and cool for 10 minutes. The skin can be removed by rubbing the foil against the beetroot, or you can take the beetroot out of the foil and rub the skin off with your hands. Do not run the beetroot under cold water as this causes the scent of the star anise to be lost. Cut beetroot into wedges.

AT THE BARBECUE

Place the beetroot package on the barbecue and cover with a wok lid or a stainless steel bowl; turn every 15 minutes. The beetroot cooks in about 45 minutes; test it with a skewer which should go easily through the whole cooked beetroot. Return the cooked beetroot to the kitchen.

AT THE TABLE

Put the salad leaves in a salad bowl and top with the beetroot wedges, grapefruit segments and pieces of goat's cheese. Mix the retained grapefruit juices with the oil and some salt; check the seasoning and then spoon over the salad. Sprinkle with croutons and serve immediately.

to

end

basics

BARBECUE BUTTERS

These butters add lots of flavour and are so easy to make. You can store them in the freezer or sometimes in the refrigerator. They are easily sliced to make a delicious topping for so many different barbecued foods.

MUSTARD AND CASHEW NUT BUTTER

250g (8oz) salted butter, at room temperature

1 tablespoon whole-grain mustard

30g (1oz) roasted and salted cashew nuts, finely crushed

1 tablespoon chopped parsley

1 tablespoon white wine vinegar

$1/_4$ teaspoon freshly ground white pepper

Put the butter, mustard and crushed nuts into a bowl and start to mash them together using a fork. Add the parsley, vinegar and pepper and continue mashing until combined and mixture is smooth.

Roll butter into a sausage shape using clingfilm or greaseproof paper and secure by twisting the ends of the clingfilm or greaseproof paper. Freeze until ready to use.

PRAWN AND LIME BUTTER

250g (8oz) salted butter

60g (2oz) cooked prawns, finely chopped

1 tablespoon finely chopped dill

1 tablespoon lime juice

1 teaspoon finely grated lime rind

Mash all ingredients together in a bowl. When well combined, place in a bowl, cover with clingfilm and refrigerate until ready to use.

HORSERADISH AND ORANGE BUTTER

250g (8oz) unsalted butter, at room temperature

2 tablespoons grated horseradish

1 tablespoon orange juice

1 teaspoon finely grated orange rind

Mash all ingredients together in a bowl until well combined. Roll into a sausage shape in clingfilm or greaseproof paper and secure by twisting the ends of the clingfilm or greaseproof paper. Freeze until ready to use.

WASABI BUTTER

250g (8oz) unsalted butter, at room temperature

1–2 teaspoons wasabi paste, or to taste

2 tablespoons finely chopped Chinese chives

1 tablespoon rice vinegar

Mash all ingredients together in a bowl until well combined. Roll into a sausage shape in clingfilm or greaseproof paper and secure by twisting the ends of the clingfilm or greaseproof paper. Freeze until ready to use.

BARBECUE TOMATO RELISH

Makes 675–900g (1^1/$_2$–2lb)

6 large, semi-ripe tomatoes

1 large onion, finely chopped

3 garlic cloves, finely chopped

2 tablespoons sugar

60ml (2fl oz) apple juice

1 tablespoon mustard powder

2 tablespoons curry powder

100ml (3fl oz) Worcestershire sauce

1 tablespoon tamarind pulp

1 bay leaf

6 whole cloves

1 small cinnamon stick

1 teaspoon salt

Remove the eyes from the bases of the tomatoes and dice roughly.

Put all ingredients, except salt, into a copper saucepan and simmer until the onion is cooked and the flavours combined, around 10 minutes, stirring constantly.

Add the salt and cook a further 5–10 minutes, stirring all the time. It is at this time that the relish can stick and burn on the bottom of the pan. Remove from the heat and discard the cinnamon stick. Cool before storing in sterilised airtight containers. Tomato relish keeps for at least 4 weeks in the refrigerator.

BASIC INDIAN SPRINKLE

This versatile sprinkle can be used to highlight the flavour of lots of barbecued goodies. I use it on fish, steaks and chicken and love what it does to potatoes and aubergines. Keep it handy and you'll come to love it like I do.

Makes 125–250g (4–8oz)

2 tablespoons ground cumin seeds
1 tablespoon salt
$3/4$ tablespoon fennel seeds
1 teaspoon garam masala
$1/2$ teaspoon paprika
$1/4$ teaspoon chilli powder

Mix all the ingredients together. Store in an airtight container and use within 7 days.

CHERMOULA

This delicious spice mix is very versatile. You often see it used with lamb or chicken, and it can also be used for prawns.

1 medium onion, very finely chopped

2 teaspoons finely chopped coriander

4 teaspoons finely chopped parsley

2 cloves garlic, crushed

4 teaspoons ground cumin seeds

2 teaspoons mild paprika

1 teaspoon ground turmeric

$1/4$ teaspoon cayenne pepper

$1/4$ teaspoon each of sea salt and ground
black pepper

Mix all the ingredients together and use as required. While Chermoula keeps in the refrigerator for up to a week, the idea with aromatic mixes is to use them as soon as they are made.

CINNAMON COURGETTE BREAD

Preheat oven to 175°C / 350°F / Gas mark 4
Makes 2 loaves

375g (12oz) small courgettes, washed,
   trimmed and grated
3 eggs, beaten with 1 tablespoon olive oil
1 tablespoon sugar
1 teaspoon ground cinnamon
1 tablespoon finely grated Parmesan cheese
$^1/_2$ teaspoon salt
375g (12oz) sifted self-raising flour
60g ($2^1/_2$oz) walnuts, crumbled
olive oil spray

Mix together the courgettes, eggs and oil, sugar, cinnamon, cheese and salt; stir to combine well. Mix in the flour and walnuts. Let mixture sit for 5 minutes.

Spray 2 bread tins (21cm (8½in) long x 11cm (4½in) wide and 10cm (4in) deep) with olive oil. Spoon equal amounts of the courgette mixture into the tins and cook in the oven for 1 hour or until a skewer comes out clean.

Leave in tins for 10 minutes then turn out onto a cooking rack to cool before slicing. (Cinnamon Courgette Bread freezes very well.)

GARLIC, WHITE WINE AND ANCHOVY CREAM

Makes 250–500ml (8fl oz–16fl oz)

2 cloves garlic, crushed
125ml (4fl oz) white wine
500ml (1 pint) single cream
1 x 40g ($1^1/_2$ oz) tin anchovies, drained
1 tablespoon coarsely chopped parsley
$^1/_4$ teaspoon cayenne pepper

Place all ingredients in a suitably sized saucepan and simmer until the mixture reduces to half its volume.

Transfer to a suitable storage container until ready to use. If refrigerated, this cream thickens and can be used as a spread for crackers or for spooning over grilled meats.

GREEN CURRY PASTE

Makes 250–375ml (8–12fl oz)

1 teaspoon cumin seeds

2 teaspoons coriander seeds

2 spring onions, trimmed, washed and
finely sliced

3 cloves garlic, peeled and roughly chopped

3cm (1in) piece galangal, peeled and
roughly chopped

1 teaspoon Thai fish sauce (*nam pla*)

6 small red chillies, deseeded and
roughly chopped

3 Kaffir lime leaves, veins removed and
finely chopped

1 teaspoon roasted shrimp paste

2 tablespoons unsalted peanuts, roughly
chopped

Dry-fry the cumin and coriander seeds over medium heat for 1 minute or until lightly browned. Cool and then grind into a powder using a mortar and pestle, or a special spice grinder.

Combine the spring onions, garlic, galangal and fish sauce in a food processor, or pound with a mortar and pestle. When a paste begins to form, add the remaining ingredients, including the cumin and coriander powder, and work into a paste.

Keep in an airtight container in the refrigerator for up to 2 days.

HOME-MADE MAYONNAISE

I always make this unique sauce by hand. While it can be made in a processor or a blender, something in the mixing motion of the balloon whisk gives Home-made Mayonnaise just that little bit extra. Once you have tried this mayonnaise, you won't want to use anything else.

Makes 250–500ml (8–16fl oz)

2 large egg yolks, at room temperature
$1/4$ teaspoon salt
pinch white pepper
$1/2$ teaspoon prepared mustard
(smooth Dijon is best)
1 teaspoon white wine vinegar
250ml (8fl oz) light olive or vegetable oil

Place the egg yolks, salt, pepper, mustard and vinegar into a clean, warmed mixing bowl.

You need to keep the bowl steady on your work bench, so secure it by wrapping a damp tea towel around its base; alternatively, ask someone to hold it in place.

With a clean balloon whisk, whisk the egg yolks and other ingredients until lightly golden in colour. Whisk in the oil slowly, drop by drop, until a third of the oil has been added.

Slowly increase the flow of oil to a thin, steady stream until all the oil has been incorporated.

If you add the oil too quickly, the mayonnaise will curdle. Should this happen, beat in 1 teaspoon of hot water and continue to add a little more oil to the mixture. When cooking with egg yolks, it's worth remembering that they cook very quickly. So if you are doing a warm egg yolk sauce, such as a Hollandaise, and the egg yolks look as though they will curdle, drop an ice cube into the mixture and continue to whisk away from the heat.

DAL (LENTIL PUREE)

Makes 450g (1lb) approximately

250g (8oz) red lentils
2 tablespoons vegetable oil
1 large onion, finely chopped
1 large clove garlic, roughly chopped
1 teaspoon finely grated root ginger
1 teaspoon ground turmeric
3 cups (24fl oz) boiling water
salt, to taste
$^1/_2$ teaspoon garam masala

Wash the lentils well and drain. Heat the oil and lightly fry the onion, garlic and ginger; add the turmeric and stir in.

Tip the lentils into the onion mixture and stir for a minute, pour in the boiling water and bring to the boil again. Reduce to a simmer and cook for 15 minutes with the lid removed or until the lentils are nearly cooked. Add the salt and garam masala and continue cooking until the mixture thickens and is breaking down. Continue stirring until all the water has evaporated.

MINT AND CHERVIL SAUCE

Makes 250–500ml (8fl oz–1 pint)

1 tablespoon finely chopped shallots

2 tablespoons fresh mint, chopped

1 tablespoon fresh chervil, chopped

1 small sprig fresh thyme

2 tablespoons white wine vinegar

2 tablespoons white wine

2 egg yolks

125 g (4oz) firm butter, cut into cubes

$1/2$ teaspoon lemon juice

salt and cayenne pepper, to taste

1 tablespoon each of fresh mint and chervil,
   torn or chopped

Make the sauce by putting the shallots, mint, chervil, thyme, vinegar and white wine into a saucepan, bring to the boil and reduce by two thirds. Remove from the heat and transfer to the top of a double boiler. Cool, add the egg yolks and whisk.

Place over simmering water and whisk until the mixture thickens; as it does, start to whisk in the butter until all is used. Remove from heat and add the lemon juice, and salt and pepper to taste. Strain and stir in finely broken or chopped mint and chervil.

NAM PRIK

You can dunk cooked prawns and freshly cut vegetables into this versatile sauce. It can also be spooned over cooked fish and used to flavour other dressings.

Makes 250ml (8fl oz) approximately

3 tablespoons dried shrimps

2 cups (16fl oz) water

1 teaspoon shrimp paste

4 cloves garlic

2 tablespoons soy sauce

2 tablespoons chilli sauce (similar to sambal olek)

2 teaspoons palm sugar

4 tablespoons water

Soak the shrimps in water for 20 minutes.

Spoon the shrimp paste onto a small piece of foil, cover with a piece of a similar size and cook under the grill or on top of the barbecue for 3 minutes or until slightly dried.

Strain the shrimps and put them and all the remaining ingredients including the dried shrimp paste into a blender and blend until smooth.

ROCKET AIOLI

Makes 250–375ml (8–12fl oz)

3 large cloves garlic

$^1/_2$ teaspoon salt, preferably sea salt

2 egg yolks

15g ($^1/_2$oz) rocket, blanched and well
    drained

1 cup (8fl oz) extra virgin olive oil

1 teaspoon lemon juice

Place the garlic, salt, egg yolks and rocket into a food processor bowl and chop or process with a chopping blade for 30 seconds.

When the mixture starts to thicken, slowly pour the oil down the feeder chute. As it mixes in, you can add the oil a little more quickly until finished.

Stir in the lemon juice just before serving. The aioli may be stored in the refrigerator for no more than 5 days — stir in the lemon juice only when you serve it.

SEMI-ROASTED TOMATO SALSA

Makes 250–500ml (8fl oz–1 pint)

150g (5oz) semi-roasted tomatoes, roughly
chopped

90g (3oz) red onion, peeled and finely
chopped

30g (1^1/$_4$oz) water chestnuts, drained and
finely diced

1 tablespoon very finely chopped green
chillies

^{1}/$_2$ teaspoon paprika

^{1}/$_2$ tablespoon brown sugar

1 tablespoon malt vinegar

2 tablespoons vegetable oil

Make this delicious salsa at least 4 hours before you plan to
use it. Just mix all the ingredients together. The salsa will store
in the refrigerator for 5 days.

SPICY BLACK-EYED BEAN PASTE

Makes 450–675g (1–1$^1/_2$lb)

250g (8oz) black-eyed beans, soaked
  and strained
4 cloves garlic, peeled and poached in water
  for 3 minutes
2 tablespoons lime juice
1 teaspoon ground cumin
1 teaspoon ground nutmeg
$^1/_2$ teaspoon ground white pepper
$^1/_4$ teaspoon chilli powder
$^1/_2$ teaspoon salt
2 tablespoons extra virgin olive oil
1 tablespoon parsley, chopped

Cook the beans, covered, in water at a simmer until they start to break down, about 40–60 minutes. Strain, and reserve 250ml (8fl oz) of the cooking liquid.

Put all the ingredients except for the oil and parsley into a food processor and reduce to a paste. You may need to add some cooking liquid to make the paste the consistency you like; it should be smooth and creamy.

Remove the paste from the processor bowl into a serving bowl and smooth over the top.

Spoon over the olive oil and sprinkle with the parsley. Serve with crusty bread or crackers.

THAI CUCUMBER SAUCE

Makes approximately 250–500ml
(8fl oz–1 pint)

4 tablespoons coconut/rice vinegar

3 tablespoons white sugar

1 small red chilli, deseeded and very finely
   chopped

1 Lebanese or ordinary cucumber, seeds
   removed and finely diced

1 shallot, finely diced

1 tablespoon grated root ginger

1 clove garlic, crushed

1 tablespoon chopped coriander

1 tablespoon vegetable oil

1 tablespoon Thai fish sauce (*nam pla*)

Mix the vinegar and sugar together and stir to dissolve.
Add all the other ingredients and marinate for 1 hour
before serving.

YOUR EVERYDAY RISOTTO

Makes 900g (1 $^3/_4$ lb)

60g (2oz) butter

1 small onion, chopped

1 clove garlic, chopped

2 tablespoons parsley, finely chopped

1 $^1/_2$ cups (11oz) arborio rice or other short-
grain risotto rice

1 litre (1 $^3/_4$ pints) boiling chicken stock

2 teaspoons salt

$^1/_2$ teaspoon white pepper

4–6 tablespoons grated Parmesan cheese

Melt 30g (1oz) of the butter in a large, heavy saucepan and pan-fry onion and garlic.

When onion is soft and golden, add parsley.

Cook over low heat for a few minutes, and add rice.

Fry for 2 minutes, stirring constantly, then add 250ml (8fl oz) of boiling stock and cook gently until all the liquid is absorbed.

Continue cooking gently, adding stock a ladleful at a time and stirring constantly, for 15–20 minutes or until rice is tender and all liquid is absorbed.

Season with salt and pepper, and stir in remaining butter and the cheese. Cover with the lid and leave risotto to sit for 3 minutes before serving.

TO SERVE

Risotto on its own tends to be somewhat bland, therefore it is an excellent accompaniment. Serve it with a little extra grated Parmesan cheese — with the addition of simple flavours, this risotto can be made into a meal.

GLOSSARY

Baharat spice: an Arabic blend of ground paprika, black pepper, cumin, coriander, cassia, cloves, green cardamom and nutmeg.

coriander: the leaves of the coriander plant are widely used.

demerara sugar: large crystals of sugar, golden in colour and made from clarified cane juice.

Désirée potato: an oval potato with smooth, pink skin and yellow flesh — partially waxy.

galangal: a stronger flavoured, more fibrous cousin to green ginger.

garam masala: a spice mixture, usually consisting of cumin, cloves, cardamom, nutmeg and pepper.

halloumi: a salty, stringy cheese from the Middle East.

julienne: to cut into very fine slices or thin strips.

Kaffir lime: the leaf of this lime tree, which has two pieces joined together; the fruit is very knobbly.

Lebanese cucumber: a short, narrow cucumber with smooth skin.

lemon pepper: cracked, lemon-flavoured peppercorns.

mesclun: mixed baby lettuce leaves.

Nigella seeds: the tiny black seeds from the Nigella tree. They are pungent with overtones of nuts and carrots.

palm sugar: a hard, dense sugar made from palm sap. Varies in colour from creamy white to dark brown.

pancetta: unsmoked, cured bacon from the belly of the pig.

panini: a flattish Italian bread, generally a small size, with a crisp exterior. Can be round or in wedges.

pide: better known as Turkish bread; full of flavour. Flat yet lumpy on the exterior, with many holes inside.

Ponzu sauce: a sour juice from the sudachy orange tree. Normally mixed with soy sauce and dashi stock.

semi-roasted tomatoes: tomatoes (usually Roma) which have been roasted for a long period at a very low temperature until they are semi-dried.

shallot: a small onion bulb, sweet and mild with thin, reddish-brown skin.

Sumac: the crushed or powdered seeds of the sumac tree. This Middle Eastern spice is delightfully tangy.

Szechuan peppercorns: berries from the prickly ash (unrelated to the peppercorn) with an intense flavour.

tahini: a smooth paste made from ground sesame seeds.

tamarind pulp: the bittersweet pulp of the fruit from a tamarind tree.

vanilla olive oil: vanilla-infused olive oil. It is available from specialist shops or through the internet.

verjuice: the non-fermented juice of tart fruits, usually apples or grapes. Semillon grapes are used frequently but other varieties can be used as well.

INDEX

First published in the UK in 2005 by
New Holland Publishers (UK) Ltd
London • Sydney • Auckland • Cape Town
www.newhollandpublishers.com

Garfield House 86–88 Edgware Road London W2 2EA United Kingdom
14 Aquatic Drive Frenchs Forest NSW 2086 Australia
218 Lake Road Northcote Auckland New Zealand
80 McKenzie Street Cape Town 8001 South Africa

2 4 6 8 10 9 7 5 3 1

ISBN: 1 84537 091 0

Managing Editor: Monica Ban
Designer: Peta Nugent
Production Manager: Linda Bottari
UK Consultant: Anna Bennett

Printer: Times Offset, Malaysia